BANKS
as ESOP Sponsors

Michael Coffey
Andrew K. Gibbs
William Gust
Corey Rosen
Jay D. Wilson, Jr.

The National Center for Employee Ownership (NCEO)
Visit us at **www.nceo.org** for more information about ESOPs

Banks as ESOP Sponsors

Michael Coffey, Andrew K. Gibbs, William Gust, Corey Rosen, and Jay D. Wilson, Jr.

Book design by Scott Rodrick

The National Center for Employee Ownership
(510) 208-1300
www.nceo.org

Published January 2023

ISBN: 978-1-954990-24-1

CONTENTS

The Popularity of Bank ESOPs

Corey Rosen

APPROXIMATELY 9% OF ALL ESOPS are in banks, the highest percentage for an NAICS (North American Industry Classification System, the standard for classifying industries in the U.S., Canada, and Mexico) subcategory. The popularity of ESOPs for banks is based on a number of benefits, including attracting and retaining employees, capital structure, and creating a market for thinly held shares.

This book starts off with an overview of how ESOPs work, including a discussion of banks as ESOP lenders. The next chapter focuses on specific issues for banks as ESOP sponsors, including a look at how ESOPs affect capital structure and accounting issues, holding company issues, regulatory requirements, and common ESOP applications. Chapter 3 explores how ESOP valuations are done for closely held banks. Finally, chapter 4 provides three case studies of banks that have implemented ESOPs. We hope this book is useful to you; see www.nceo.org for more information on ESOPs, employee ownership, and creating an ownership culture.

CHAPTER ONE

Banks as ESOP Sponsors: An Overview of How ESOPs Work

Corey Rosen

"Once each owner-employee understands that they own a piece of the company, then their thought processes and behaviors change. Our record of steady, profitable, and growing performance over time supports that belief. Happy owner-employees tend to remain with the bank, thus reducing recruitment and training expense. Our combined ESOP and 401(k) plan now has even created some employee-owner millionaires."

— Joe Frampton, CEO, Paducah Bank and Trust

THIS BOOK DISCUSSES BANKS as sponsors of employee stock ownership plans (ESOPs). This chapter provides an overview. Later chapters address the details of finance, valuation, and special issues for banks, and chapter 2 ("Special Issues for Banks as ESOP Sponsors") delves more deeply into the nuts and bolts of ESOP operations.

There are about 600 banks with ESOPs, meaning that about 9% of all ESOPs are in banks, the highest percentage for any industry. This book explains why banks find ESOPs attractive, what the rules are for ESOPs, the many tax benefits of an ESOP, how ESOPs can be used to provide a market for shares of other owners, and the special regulatory considerations for banks as ESOP sponsors.

Banks, of course, can also be lenders to ESOPs. While that is not the focus of this book, it will help you understand why making loans to ESOPs may be very a good business for your bank. A study by the National Center for Employee Ownership (NCEO) covering the period between 2009 and 2013 found that the default rate (defined as imposing losses on creditors) on bank loans to ESOPs was just two per thousand per year. Often, banks find that if they help a company become an ESOP, they also become that company's banker for other purposes.

Looking at the most recent (2020) data on bank ESOPs as reported to and released by the U.S. Department of Labor (DOL) shows that:

- Bank ESOP companies collectively employ 656,000 active participants (those employed and currently in the plan) and 956,000 total participants (this includes those who have left the company but not yet received a complete distribution of their accounts).
- The average bank ESOP has 1,100 active participants; the median-sized bank ESOP has 86 active participants.
- While a very small number of banks are 100% owned by their ESOP, the typical bank ESOP owns between about 5% and 25% of the company's shares. That is different from non-bank ESOPs, where the plans usually own at least 30% of the stock and most often 100%.
- One-third of the banks are organized as S corporations and the rest as C corporations.
- ESOPs in banks hold a total of $16.1 billion in company stock. Participants have an average of $27,500 in company stock per participant. Account values grow over time. More senior employees would have much larger account balances, but the data reported to the DOL does not allow for this level of analysis.

Successful ESOPs help reduce turnover, improve customer interaction, generate ideas from employees, and provide an added appeal to many customers—in fact, polling shows that the large majority of people prefer to patronize employee-owned companies. Just setting up a plan is not enough, however. As the case studies in this book show, successful ESOP companies communicate regularly about the ESOP and the bank with employee-owners and provide them with ways to share and implement their ideas. Done well, ESOPs can be a win for everyone. In fact, ESOP companies grow about 2.5% per year faster with an ESOP than would have been expected without one.

To illustrate the potential benefits to having an ESOP for a bank, for this book Andy Gibbs and Jay Wilson of Mercer Capital analyzed the historical performance of banks with ESOPs relative to those without ESOPs over the last twenty years (2002–2021). Figure 1-1 shows, ESOP banks outperformed non-ESOP banks, particularly in the last decade. The median return on average equity (ROAE) for a bank with an ESOP from 2002 to 2021 was 9.90%, approximately 98 basis points (BPS) above banks without ESOPs at 8.92%. The median return on average assets (ROAA) for a bank with an ESOP from 2002 to 2021 was 1.01%, approximately 4 BPS above banks without ESOPs at 0.97%.

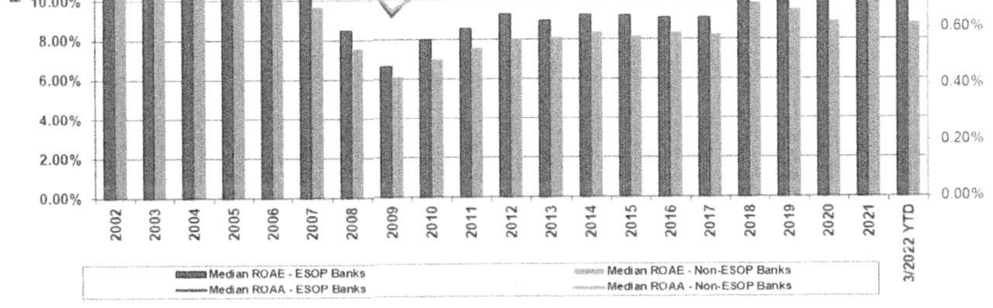

Figure 1-1. Profitability trends

(Data derived from Call Report filings and S&P Global Market Intelligence; historical comparison of 544 banks with ESOPs and 4,193 banks without ESOPs. S corporation bank earnings were tax-effected to be comparable to C corporation bank earnings.)

Later chapters in this book focus on special issues for bank ESOP sponsors. This chapter explains the rules, tax benefits, and financing of ESOPs in general.

What Is an ESOP?

An ESOP is an employee benefit plan designed to invest primarily in the stock of the employer. The stock must be common stock, although preferred stock convertible to common can be used. ESOPs are governed by the Employee Retirement Income Security Act (ERISA), the same law that regulates many aspects of 401(k) plans, profit sharing plans, pension plans, and health and welfare plans, and the Internal Revenue Code (the "Code"). The rules for ESOPs are on many issues the same as those for other retirement plans, although it is better to think of ESOPs as wealth-building plans that are part of an overall retirement plan structure.

To use an ESOP, a company sets up an ESOP trust, much like any other retirement plan trust. While it is possible for employees to buy shares through the trust, this is not common and occurs almost entirely in public companies. Instead, employers fund the plan with tax-deductible contributions of shares or cash to buy shares. Unique among retirement plans, ESOPs can borrow money to buy shares, with the company making contributions to the trust to repay the loan. This allows the ESOP to buy substantial blocks of stock, the release the shares to employee accounts as the loan is repaid.

Why Companies Set Up ESOPs

There are about 6,500 ESOPs, 90% of which are in closely held companies. ESOPs can be used for a variety of purposes:

- The most common use of an ESOP is to provide liquidity for an owner or owners of a closely held company. Many owners of these companies could sell to another company or to a private equity form, but are not comfortable with the legacy implications of that. The new buyer may move the company to another area, reduce employment as it consolidates functions, change the name, and limit or eliminate any role for the selling owner or owners. Often, the owners also feel a responsibility to reward the people who helped them build the company. Selling to an ESOP provides a tax-favored, practical way to sell part or all of the owners' interests while preserving the legacy of the business and allowing the sellers to retain any role they choose going forward. Using a plan this way probably accounts for about 75% of ESOPs. Most of these ESOPs will end up owning 100% of the shares, although often that will happen over several years and two or more transactions.

- In public companies, ESOPs are most often used as a match to the company's 401(k) plan. Companies may see that as less costly than contributing cash. Companies may also choose to do this because dividends paid on ESOP shares are tax-deductible and/or because they think that having employees own company stock may provide additional motivation. These ESOPs usually own 5% or less of a company's stock.
- Some closely held companies use ESOPs primarily as a reward for employees and as part of an effort to create an employee ownership culture. Owners may not be looking to transition out any time soon, although down the road, they often see ESOPs as an option to consider.

Bank ESOPs can have all these elements. ESOPs provide a market for shares of owners, something that may be especially appealing when there are many minority owners who might otherwise have limited liquidity options. Banks also commonly use the ESOP as a match for their 401(k) plans, and most of the time they see ESOPs as a way to engage employees and improve employee retention.

Tax Benefits of ESOPs

ESOPs have substantial tax benefits:

- *Contributions to the ESOP are tax-deductible.* Banks can use these contributions to buy newly issued shares in pretax dollars, dollars that both fund a benefit and increase bank common equity (this topic is explored in more detail later in this book). Alternatively, the ESOP can purchase shares from existing owners, again in pretax dollars. Normally, this kind of redemption is done with after-tax dollars. For instance, a $1 million redemption might require $1.5 million in pretax income; with an ESOP, just $1 million is required.

- *ESOPs can borrow money to buy shares.* When the company repays the loan through the ESOP, it deducts both the interest and the principal, not just the interest. The ESOP can do this to buy existing shares or newly issued shares. For instance, the ESOP can use the loan proceeds to buy newly issued shares, and the company can use the proceeds from the sale of those shares for capital acquisitions that would otherwise be financed with debt that only generates a tax deduction for interest payments. The ESOP also can use the loan proceeds to buy a larger block of stock and allocate them over time as it repays the loan.
- *In S corporation ESOPs, earnings attributable to the ESOP trust are not taxable.* If an S corporation ESOP, for instance, is 20% owned by the ESOP trust, then 20% of the profits are not taxable. If the company makes distributions, however, the trust must get a pro-rata share of these distributions. The trust can use these to buy more shares, keep in reserve to buy back shares from employees after they leave, or just to add to employee assets.
- *Dividends paid on ESOP shares in C corporations are tax-deductible* if used to repay a loan or passed through to employees.
- *Finally, sellers to ESOPs that are in closely held C corporations (or in S corporations in 2028 and later to a very limited extent),*[1] *including companies that convert to C status at the time of the sale, can reinvest ("roll over") the proceeds in stock and bonds of U.S. operating companies and defer tax* on the gains under Code Section 1042 until the replacement securities are sold.

Rules for Using the Section 1042 Rollover

As mentioned above, one of the major benefits of an ESOP for closely held C corporations is found in Section 1042 of the Internal Revenue

1. Starting in 2028, owners of S corporations selling to a qualifying ESOP can defer 10% of the gain.

Code. Under it, a seller to an ESOP may qualify for a deferral of taxation on the gain made from the sale. Several requirements apply, the most significant of which are:

1. The seller must have held the stock for three years before the sale.
2. The stock must not have been acquired through stock options or other employee benefit plans.
3. The ESOP must own 30% or more of the value of the company's shares and must continue to hold this amount for three years unless the company is sold. Shares the company repurchases from departing employees do not count. Stock sold in a transaction that brings the ESOP to 30% of the total shares qualifies for the deferral treatment.
4. Shares qualifying for the deferral cannot be allocated to the accounts of the selling shareholder(s); to lineal descendants, brothers or sisters, spouses, or parents of the selling shareholder(s); or to any more-than-25% shareholders.

If these rules are met, the seller (or sellers) can take the proceeds from the sale (up to 100% for C corporations and 10% for S corporations in 2028 onward) and reinvest them in "qualified replacement property" during the period running from 3 months before to 12 months after the sale and defer any capital gains tax until these new investments are sold, at which time the basis is the owner's original basis in the ESOP company's shares. Qualified replacement property essentially means stocks, bonds, warrants, or debentures of domestic corporations receiving not more than 25% of their income from passive investment. Mutual funds and real estate trusts do not qualify. If the replacement securities are held until death, they are subject to a step-up in basis at that time, so capital gains taxes would never be paid.

Financing

The simplest way to finance an ESOP to transfer ownership is to have the company make tax-deductible cash contributions to the ESOP trust, which the trust then uses to gradually purchase the owner's shares.

The company can also just issue new shares. Alternatively, the owner can have the ESOP borrow the funds needed to buy the shares. In this way, larger amounts of stock can be purchased all at once, up to 100% of the equity. Normally, a bank will loan to the company, which then reloans to the ESOP, not necessarily on the same terms.

Perhaps half of all ESOPs, however, are funded instead by a seller note, sometimes with warrants as part of the deal (see more details on this below). The ESOP acquires the shares and then pays back the seller at a reasonable rate of interest (not more than what a commercial lender would charge for loans of similar risk.) Sellers often like this idea because not only do they get their shares sold, but they get a reasonably good rate of return on the note. In this scenario, however, the tax-deferred rollover would apply only to what is reinvested within twelve months of the sale date. The entire amount of the sale could only be reinvested, therefore, if the seller has other funds available or, as normally happens, the seller borrows money from a bank to buy special ESOP bonds that qualify for this kind of sale (a common approach). The seller then repays the banks with the proceeds of the note. However the money is obtained, the price is set by an independent appraiser, as discussed below.

How the Price the Selling Owner Receives Is Determined

The price the ESOP pays for the shares, as well as any other purchases by the plan, must be determined at least annually by an outside, independent appraiser unless there is a public market for the shares.[2] The appraiser's valuation will be based on several factors. Most ap-

2. The SECURE 2.0 Act of 2022, enacted as part of the Consolidated Appropriations Act of 2023, appeared to intend to extend the definition of "publicly traded" to include securities that are subject to priced quotations by at least four dealers on an SEC-regulated interdealer quotation system, are not a penny stock, are not issued by a shell company, and have a public float of at least 10% of outstanding shares. Domestic issuers must publish audited financial statements at least annually, and foreign issuers have additional requirements.

   Unfortunately, the bill contains what appears to be a drafting error in what part of the tax code it amends, so this will become effective only if Congress makes a technical correction to the act in 2024 or 2025.

praisers try to find comparable public companies and use their price/earnings ratio, price/assets ratio, and other guides for setting a price. Discounted cash flow, book value, the company's reputation, future market considerations, and other factors will be considered as well, and often are the most heavily weighted factor. The appraiser will try, as much as possible, to determine how much the business would be worth if there were a market for it. The appraiser is assessing what a financial buyer would pay, one who would operate the business as a stand-alone entity. A strategic buyer, such as a competitor, by contrast, might pay an additional premium because when the target company is acquired, there are perceived operational synergies that make the target more profitable to the buyer than it would be as a stand-alone entity. The ESOP cannot match this price because it cannot generate these synergies. Sales to synergistic buyers do trigger capital gains taxes, however, and often come with numerous contingencies.

If a bank is publicly traded on a stock exchange or over the counter, the share price established by the market is used instead of a valuation.

How Employees Get Stock

ESOPs are much like other tax-qualified retirement plans. At least all employees who have worked at least 1,000 hours in a plan year must be included. They receive allocations of shares in the ESOP based on relative pay or a more level formula. Pay over the annual ERISA cap on eligible pay ($330,000 as of 2023) does not count. If there is an ESOP loan, the shares are allocated each year based on the percentage of the loan that is repaid that year. The allocations are subject to vesting for as long as six years. Employees do not receive a distribution of shares until they terminate, and then the distribution can be delayed for five years after the end of the plan year they leave if for reasons other than death, retirement, or disability. If it is for one of those reasons, distributions start one year after the end of the plan year the event occurs. Distributions can be made in installments of stock or cash over a five-year period, with interest if made in cash. Employees have the right to sell the shares back to the company at the appraised value.

Once an employee has been in the plan for at least 10 years and has reached the age of 55 or older, the employee can elect to diversify up to 25% of the shares in their account, and up to another 25% five years later.

It is important to understand that ESOPs do not allow employers to pick and choose who can get stock or to make allocations based on discretionary decisions. It is also critical to remember that ESOPs do not as a rule entail employees using their own money to buy shares. The company funds the plan. The ESOP trust holds the shares, and the ESOP trustee is the shareholder of record for the company stock in the plan; the participants are beneficial owners who have accounts in the ESOP.

Governance and Fiduciary Issues

The plan is governed by a trustee appointed by the board; employees only have very limited required voting rights (they do not have to elect the board, for instance), although companies may provide additional rights. The most important of these issues is the sale of all or substantially all of the assets of the plan; stock sales do not require a pass-through vote.

It is highly advisable (and the DOL believes it is always advisable) for any transaction between the ESOP trust and a seller to be overseen and approved by an outside, independent trustee. The trustee hires the appraisal firm, who works for the trustee, not the seller or the company (and, in fact, has not even had prior engagements with either). Ongoing ESOP operations, including the repurchase of shares from former employees, bring less urgency to having an outside trustee. Somewhat more than half of all ESOP companies instead create an inside trustee or trustee committee.

Advisory Team and Costs

All ESOP transactions need an outside appraisal firm, a trustee, an attorney for the trust, and an attorney for the company; many transactions add someone to do a feasibility analysis and/or provide financial structuring advice or assistance.

This can all be very expensive, with fees ranging from between $100,000 and $500,000 for most transactions. That makes ESOPs out of reach for smaller companies (usually fewer than 20 employees) or any company without sufficient profits to pay the fees and pay the cost of buying the new shares and still have finds to operate profitably. It should be noted, though, that sales to ESOPs are usually not more complicated or expensive (and have fewer contingencies) than sales to other buyers.

Accounting

If the company contributes new shares of stock, the value of the shares at the time of the contribution is counted as a compensation expense. The par value of the shares is credited to common stock par value, while paid-in capital is credited at the difference between par value and current fair market value.

If the contribution is in cash and used to buy existing shares, the value of the contribution is charged to compensation expense, while cash is credited with the value of the contribution.

Footnote disclosures in either case should identify the plan and the employee groups covered, describe the company's contribution policy, and identify how much was contributed when.

Employer contributions to repay an ESOP loan are counted as compensation expense and repayment of interest. The repayment of interest is measured as it would be for any other loan. Compensation expense is more complicated. At its simplest, compensation expense would equal the amount of principal paid on the loan in any year. However, ESOP sponsors also can allocate shares using the principal-plus-interest method. This has resulted in loans structured with unusual amortization schedules. Compensation expense equals:

Shares allocated for the period ÷ total shares purchased
× original principal
+ interest expense
– dividends

The ESOP loan debt is recorded as a "contra-equity" account that diminishes over time as the loan is repaid. This can create negative tangible net worth, at least in accounting terms. Lenders need to assess this and set appropriate covenants.

Creating an Ownership Culture

By far the most successful ESOPs are those that create effective ownership cultures. That means:

- Sharing overall corporate financial information with employees
- Sharing metrics about elements of company performance
- Training people in both work and business skills
- Getting employees involved, individually and in teams, in making more decisions about their jobs

ESOP companies typically set up a team of nonmanagement employees to provide regular communication about the plan and the company through events, newsletters, FAQs, email updates, and more. They also often have an idea team to steer employee involvement. This can include setting up employee workgroups, functional teams, cross-functional teams, ad hoc teams to address a specific issue, and more. The case studies in this book explain how ESOP-owned banks have done this.

Banks as ESOP Lenders

There are good reasons for banks to get involved as ESOP lenders. As noted earlier, ESOP loans are very safe debt. They also are a way for banks to retain or attract company business for other services and help keep the companies in the community.

Loans to companies to fund an ESOP are largely like loans for any other leveraged buyouts, but with some important wrinkles. First, as noted earlier, the company can deduct principal and interest on the loan if it is less than a 100% ESOP purchase. If it is a 100% purchase, and the company is or becomes an S corporation, then there are effectively no taxes paid because the ESOP, unlike other S owners, is not required to pay taxes on its share of company profits. In either case, then, the company is in a better position to repay the loan than would be the case with a non-ESOP loan to buy company shares or assets. Second, in some ESOP deals, the company is looking to buy back a minority interest and has enough collateral so that a bank loan can be fully collateralized. But if the company is looking to have the ESOP buy 100% of the company, as is often the case, seller notes are added, and sometimes mezzanine and/or unitranche debt, to supplement the bank loan. Some of these seller notes involve warrants. Finally, some loans for ESOP purchases require the seller to pledge the qualified replacement property the seller may acquire. The collateral is released as the loan is repaid.

Warrants provide the holder the right to the value of a stated number shares at a price fixed at the time of sale, either the transaction price or the post-transaction price (which will be lower because of the debt). The seller agrees to forego some of the interest that a reasonably priced note would entail (usually three to seven points above the bank rate) in exchange for the right to the warrants. A financial advisor will calculate what the exchange rate should be, and the ESOP trustee must approve it as fair to the participants.

After the transaction, banks may impose covenants on loans similar to any leveraged transaction, including for debt coverage ratios and sometimes specific uses of funds.

Table 1-1 looks at how the various components of debt are often structured.

Table 1-1. Debt structure components of an ESOP transaction*

Form of debt	Term	Rate	Collateral requirements
Senior debt	Three to seven years	Libor + 1.5%–3.0%	Strict
Unitranche debt (blended senior+ mezzanine debt)	Five to seven years	Libor + 7.5%–9.0%	Less strict
Mezzanine debt	Five years	Libor + 10%–13%	Flexible
Structured equity	Five years	10%–13% plus warrants	Flexible

*These numbers are based on a presentation at an NCEO conference in 2022 by Steve Ryan of GreatBanc Trust Company.

Structured equity is used only in the largest deals, and even then only in a very small number cases (a few to several a year). Mezzanine or unitranche debt is used in perhaps 10% of transactions, again more commonly in larger deals.

Conclusion

ESOPs can be a powerful tool for attracting, retaining, and motivating employees; providing a market for your bank's stock; and improving company performance. There is a reason they are so common in banks. This book will help you explore whether they are right for yours.

CHAPTER TWO

Special Issues for Banks as ESOP Sponsors

Michael Coffey and William Gust[1]

THE ESOP IS AN IMPORTANT TOOL for managing a variety of issues facing banks. Banks proportionately make more use of ESOPs than any other industrial classification in the U.S., often without understanding the extent of their potential applications. While an ESOP is not suitable in all circumstances, an ESOP may provide assistance in resolving the following issues, either by itself or in conjunction with other elements of a well-rounded strategic plan:

- *Augmenting capital,* particularly for profitable institutions facing limited access to external capital. Though an ESOP strategy generally builds capital more slowly than a private placement alternative or a public offering, it provides certain tax advantages and may result in less dilution to existing shareholders.
- *Facilitating stock purchases* by creating an internal stock market. The ESOP offers the further advantage of providing a vehicle to own shares that is "friendly" to the existing board of directors.

---

1. *Editor's note:* This chapter is an adaptation of material from *The ESOP Handbook for Banks* by Corporate Capital Resources and Mercer Capital (Peabody Publishing, 2011). We thank Mercer Capital and Peabody Publishing for providing us permission to use this material for this book.

- *Providing employee benefits.* ESOPs provide a beneficial tool in rewarding employees who add to the institution's long-term value.

ESOPs are subject to both tax and benefit (qualified plan) law provisions, which were first spelled out formally for ESOPs in the Employee Retirement Income Security Act of 1974 (ERISA).

The best decision tree will have a competent feasibility study performed to reduce the complexity to manageable proportions. ESOP implementation can be a complex process when viewed from a technical perspective. It need not be so complex when understood as part of a *coordinated* capitalization or market-making strategy. An ESOP alone is never *the* answer to a bank's strategy decisions, and ESOPs should not be installed without due appreciation of the need to coordinate the plan with key executive compensation, the selling shareholders' desires, employee benefit limits, and a host of other concerns.

The need for strategic clarity may be illustrated by an anecdote based on our many years of working with ESOPs. In this example, an ESOP was rejected as a planning option, though it could have been part of a good solution to the bank's needs: An officer of a bank holding company was interested in making a tax-efficient market for a class of preferred stock other than the existing common stock and was told by a tax attorney that the ESOP could only purchase the highest and best class of shares with respect to voting rights, dividend preferences, and other features. While the "highest and best class" rule was correct and required, the counsel failed to suggest a broader strategy. The holding company could sell newly issued common shares to the ESOP (which would be dilutive to per-share value), gain a tax deduction for the purchase by the ESOP, and then use untaxed proceeds from the common stock sale to redeem some preferred shares (offsetting the dilution caused by the sale of stock to the ESOP). This process is at times referred to as "going public internally." In this case, the process could have been executed with minimal dilution. This strategy for the closely held holding company would have required an independent valuation of the common stock and a coordinated plan, but would have provided the desired result: the redemption of preferred stock with pretax dollars using the ESOP as a single, tax-exempt shareholder.

This chapter describes the function of ESOPs in the real world of banks and bank holding companies. While it can correct misunderstandings and offer sound guidance, it cannot exhaustively detail the many interactions of ESOPs with current federal and state banking regulations and the extensive laws and regulations governing employee benefits and taxation. Bank directors and managers can use the information in this chapter to make solid initial decisions regarding the potential merits of an ESOP.

Those directors and managers who make decisions affecting bank profitability, ownership, and capitalization should be aware of the potential advantages of an ESOP in offering a tax-advantaged vehicle that supports local control while building shareholder value. This approach may prove beneficial compared with alternative structures that bring outside capital to the table for a price exacted in terms of greater dilution, dollars, and at times, control. Both approaches must be considered by any board of directors.

Before embarking on a particular strategy to deal with the various challenges facing small- to mid-size banks, the decision-makers in profitable institutions may wish to consider how an ESOP can assist in addressing issues such as shareholder liquidity, employee ownership and compensation, and capital management.

While every case is unique with respect to specific combinations of corporate objectives, employee benefit goals, tax concerns, and the like, the following considerations can help bank officers evaluate the potential benefit of implementing an ESOP:

- A bank or a bank holding company that is a C or an S corporation can sponsor an ESOP, but it must be sufficiently profitable to take advantage of the tax benefits derived from contributions of stock or cash to the plan; corporations with less than $500,000 of pretax, pre-benefit plan earnings are questionable candidates.
- The bank must have enough employees to meet the various contribution limit and other tests required for compliance with rules under the Internal Revenue Code (the "Code"). ESOPs have been implemented in companies with fewer than 20 to 30 employees, but this is not recommended. An eligible payroll for qualified plan purposes of over $1 million is generally the threshold.

- Both publicly traded and private banks can sponsor ESOPs, but actively traded institutions typically do not need the market for bank stock that can be generated by an ESOP. Private and thinly traded banks often need the market for shares and make the greatest use of these plans. The most appropriate strategies and applicable rules governing ESOP operation differ considerably for private and public companies.
- Stock must be available within a few years of plan installation for either contribution to the ESOP or for purchase by the ESOP. The ESOP is indifferent to the source of the shares—newly issued shares or stock from outside shareholders—but because the ESOP is an economic buyer, it can purchase the shares at no more than fair market value. This stock value must be determined by an independent appraisal firm at the time of purchase when the bank or bank holding company is closely held or thinly traded.
- The financial strength of the bank should be sufficient over time to support shareholder value. Contra-indications of a strong ESOP candidate include erratic or low earnings, inadequate capital ratios relative to regulatory expectations, poor CAMELS ratings,[2] and other negative factors known to management (e.g., pending detrimental litigation), It is important to remember that ESOPs are long-term retirement plans with an interest in the long-term economic viability of the bank sponsor.
- A psychological factor is also important for management to consider. Bank management must be willing to engage in the process of managing not just cash flows, capital ratios, regulatory requirements, and the like, but also the interaction and effect of stock flows between the bank/bank holding company, shareholders, and the ESOP. Such complexity can accomplish corporate objectives, but nonetheless requires effort and a clear understanding of the strategies involved.
- A corollary of the ESOP "psychology" is the establishment of an ownership culture among the bank's employee base. Employees

2. Rating given by the Federal Deposit Insurance Corporation (FDIC) and other bank supervisors to monitor the health of individual banks, based on financials and on-site examinations. The acronym stands for *C*apital adequacy, *A*sset quality, *M*anagement quality, *E*arnings, *L*iquidity, and *S*ensitivity to market risk.

should be educated as to their influence on the value being created in the plan's stockholdings, and greater financial transparency may be necessary. It is important to emphasize that while the ESOP participants have an economic interest in the value created, they are "beneficial" rather than the legal owners of plan-held stock. The legal owners of the shares are the trustees of the plan, who are appointed by the board of directors.

Using an ESOP to Enhance Capital

One of the benefits of an ESOP is the bank's ability to raise additional capital by making tax-deductible contributions to the ESOP, which are then used to purchase shares of stock from the sponsoring company. For example, a bank could contribute $100 to an ESOP, which because of the tax deductibility of the contribution, results in an after-tax expense of only $65 (assuming a 35% tax rate). Shortly thereafter, the ESOP can purchase $100 of newly issued common shares, increasing the bank's common equity by $100 at an after-tax cost of $65. While an ESOP has its benefits as part of a capital strategy, it also has its limitations.

- The benefits provided by the ESOP structure are realized gradually. If the bank or bank holding company requires an immediate capital infusion, the ESOP is not the best solution, although it can be used in conjunction with other capital-raising strategies.
- Quantitative limits exist on the amount the employer may contribute to the plan, thereby capping the capital enhancement and tax benefits derived from ESOP contributions.
- The strategy requires the bank or bank holding company to be profitable (or at least to record a book tax benefit, if it reports a book loss) to realize the tax benefits.
- The shares purchased by the ESOP must one day be repurchased from the plan in order to provide sufficient cash to find the retirement benefit for participants. These repurchase obligations can become significant issues for plans holding a more substantial share of the employer's outstanding common stock and should be managed carefully.

Example of an ESOP Transaction

To illustrate the benefits of using an ESOP as a capital-raising tool, we present a simple example of a bank that installs an ESOP for the benefit of its employees with the goal of using tax-deductible contributions to the plan eventually to redeem some outstanding holding company stock. While we present specific numbers below, we emphasize the general impact on bank capital ratios, cash flows, stock value, and ownership transition.

XYZ Bancorp

For this example, consider a healthy financial institution, XYZ Bancorp. The holding company's primary asset is its investment in XYZ Bank, and it incurs minimal operating expenses. At December 31, 2022, both the bank and the holding company are well-capitalized, but management of XYZ Bancorp has set a goal to make a market for some of its stock and provide an opportunity for bank employees to benefit from the growth in stock value as a result of their efforts.

Additionally, XYZ Bank has a management team that is nearing retirement age and that owns a meaningful percentage of the holding company's closely held shares. After evaluating a number of options, the management team determines that installing an ESOP is the most tax-effective way to accumulate cash with which to acquire stock, thereby transitioning ownership to the next generation of employee/managers while also facilitating the repurchase of shares held by the existing management team.

ESOP Transaction

The ESOP is installed effective January 1, 2023, and the bank makes tax-deductible ESOP contributions of $1,666,000 in 2023, 2024, and 2025. The ESOP, in turn, accumulates these cash contributions until 2025, when it purchases $5 million of newly issued common shares in XYZ Bancorp. As the last step in this transaction, XYZ Bancorp redeems the preferred stock investment with the funds provided by the ESOP's purchase of newly issued common shares.

The contribution, which is significant at approximately 25% of covered compensation, causes XYZ Bank's return on assets to decline by about 20% during the 2023 to 2025 period, versus a scenario where no ESOP is implemented, assuming the bank makes no offsetting adjustments to any existing benefit plans. From a capital standpoint, we compared XYZ Bank's equity/asset ratio in 2025, assuming ESOP implementation occurs, to an alternative scenario that does not establish an ESOP but assumes a $5 million dividend from the bank to the holding company. In this comparison, XYZ Bank's 2025 equity/asset ratio is about 3% higher if XYZ Bank uses an ESOP.

In 2025, the ESOP purchases shares of the company's common stock at the fair market value of the stock as determined by an independent appraiser. The shares purchased by the ESOP in 2025 are newly issued by the company, raising the additional capital necessary for management in turn to redeem the preferred stock. An important issue for the ESOP's independent appraiser to consider is the extent to which XYZ Bank's contributions leading up to the ESOP's share purchase are indicative of its ongoing contribution levels. The example assumes that the ESOP starts with a contribution level of 25% of eligible pay per year but then normalizes to 10% of compensation soon after the transaction. Based on this assumption, the total number of shares outstanding increases by approximately 9% in our example, and the ESOP now holds around an 8% stake in the company, but the CPP preferred stock has been redeemed and the dividend payment obligation extinguished without raising external capital.

Why would management and the board of directors determine that such dilution to earnings, capital ratios, and ownership is an acceptable result? In short, it would reach this conclusion if these outcomes compare favorably relative to the alternatives available:

- Relative to a scenario where no ESOP is installed, but XYZ Bank provides a dividend of $5 million to enable XYZ Bancorp to redeem the CPP preferred stock, the ESOP scenario results in greater capital at the bank and holding company. This additional capital approximates the tax benefit of the ESOP contributions.
- Investor groups unaffiliated with the holding company may require substantial concessions to encourage their investment, which may

be dilutive to remaining shareholders (e.g., warrants in addition to the shares purchased). While an ESOP can pay no more than fair market value for the shares, it may be viewed as a more friendly vehicle to acquire shares than a private investor group.

Alternative to an ESOP

As an alternative to installing an ESOP, XYZ Bancorp management may raise additional capital in a private placement transaction. Assuming no other changes to financial performance, management may expect the private placement to result in greater dilution of the common stock. For example, existing shareholders and directors may not have the financial means or desire to make substantial additional capital injections. In this case, the bank holding company may turn to an investor group to raise the necessary capital; however, smaller banks often attract less interest from these groups, who often look for attractive public offering or acquisition candidates. With a less persuasive exit strategy, the investor group may demand greater concessions on price, transaction enhancements such as warrants, and other nonfinancial perquisites such as board of directors' seats. Based on these requirements from investor groups, management may reasonably expect that the number of shares the ESOP would need to purchase to raise enough capital to redeem would be smaller than the number of shares that would need to be sold in a private placement.

In the example, we assumed that XYZ Bancorp issues stock in a private placement at an approximate 15% discount to the shares' fair market value, as would be used in an ESOP transaction. If this occurs, then the bank holding company would issue more shares to the investors in the private placement than it would have issued to an ESOP, creating greater dilution for all the shareholders. Depending on the ongoing ESOP contribution, by implementing an ESOP the bank holding company could have higher earnings per share than if it undertook a private placement and provided its employees with an additional retirement benefit.

Scenario Comparison

Tables 2-1 through 2-4 summarize key metrics for XYZ Bank under the four scenarios described above. All scenarios assume the same growth and profitability expectations (ROAA = return on average assets; ROAE = return on average equity).

Table 2-1. Do-nothing scenario

	2022	2023	2024	2025
Earnings				
ROAA	.97%	1.00%	1.00%	1.00%
ROAE	9.92%	9.91%	9.46%	9.08%
Consolidated net income (in thousands)	$5,525	$5,801	$6,091	$6,396
Performance metrics				
Earnings per share	$100	$105	$110	$116
Book value per share	$931	$1,026	$1,125	$1,129
Shares outstanding	55,250	55,250	55,250	55,250

Table 2-2. Bank dividend scenario

	2022	2023	2024	2025
Earnings				
ROAA	.97%	1.00%	1.00%	1.00%
ROAE	9.92%	9.91%	9.46%	9.44%
Consolidated net income (in thousands)	$5,525	$5,801	$6,091	$6,396
Performance metrics				
Earnings per share	$100	$105	$110	$116
Book value per share	$931	$1,026	$1,125	$1,139
Shares outstanding	55,250	55,250	55,250	55,250

Table 2-3. ESOP scenario

	2022	2023	2024	2025
Earnings				
ROAA	.97%	.79%	.80%	.81%
ROAE	9.92%	7.98%	7.86%	7.74%
Consolidated net income (in thousands)	$5,525	$4,718	$5,008	$5,313
Performance metrics				
Earnings per share	$100	$85	$91	$91
Book value per share	$931	$1,007	$1,086	$1,072
Shares outstanding	55,250	55,250	55,250	60,342

Table 2-4. Private placement scenario

	2022	2023	2024	2025
Earnings				
ROAA	.97%	1.00%	1.00%	.94%
ROAE	9.92%	9.91%	9.46%	8.60%
Consolidated net income (in thousands)	$5,525	$5,801	$6,091	$6,396
Performance metrics				
Earnings per share	$100	$105	$110	$110
Book value per share	$931	$1,026	$1,125	$1,108
Shares outstanding	55,250	55,250	55,250	61,017

The ESOP Going Forward

Once the bank has used the cash held by the ESOP to raise capital with which to redeem the CPP preferred stock, the ESOP can be used to buy out existing shareholders desiring liquidity. XYZ Bancorp pays annual dividends on its common stock, resulting in dividends paid to the ESOP, which can be deductible if used to repay an ESOP loan or passed through to participants. Additionally, management can continue to make contributions to the ESOP. The dividends and the ongoing contributions result in cash inflows for the ESOP, which, coupled with any cash remaining after the redemption, leaves the ESOP with cash available to purchase additional shares in later years, increasing the ownership percentage. Keep in mind that the shares purchased after 2025 are obtained from existing shareholders, and the only dilution occurs in 2025, with the issuance of new stock to redeem.

This can continue indefinitely (or at least until the ESOP owns 100% of the company), with the company varying the amount of contributions and dividends depending upon the amount of shares the ESOP wishes to purchase, the financial performance of the bank, and the liquidity needs of other shareholders. The contributions are deductible for tax purposes, while the dividends may be deductible depending on how they are used. Shareholders who are not participants in the ESOP are able to receive dividends, but they cannot able to participate in the contributions. Management must take into consideration the need to balance the return to all ownership classes of the company. Additionally, all else equal, the contributions do result in a decline in earnings in the years in which they are made, and the reduced earnings must be balanced with the benefits of creating liquidity for shareholders and increasing the ESOP's ownership interest.

Additional Considerations

The example above involving XYZ Bancorp made a number of simplifying assumptions for illustrative purposes. In reality, additional complexities enter into any analysis of whether an ESOP satisfies a company's objectives. Some of these additional considerations include:

- If net income is depressed leading up to the ESOP transaction as the company builds a "cash warehouse" by making periodic ESOP contributions, the stock value at the time of the transaction may be reduced, reflecting the depressed earnings. However, depending on the specific facts and circumstances, an appraiser may not consider the amount of such contributions to be reflective of the company's actual expense structure and may factor this consideration into the determination of the company's stock value at the time of the transaction. Some add-back of plan contributions in excess of peer-group retirement plan contributions is common when arriving at a representative earnings base for a valuation.
- The example shown here pertaining to XYZ Bancorp shows a decline in earnings in the years in which the ESOP contributions occur, reflecting an increase in personnel expenses in the amount of the contributions. In some situations, the increase in expenses may not be as significant. Because ESOP contributions represent an employee benefit, banks with ESOPs may consider reducing contributions to other retirement plans or may otherwise reduce certain personnel expenses as an offset to the ESOP contribution. The extent to which ESOP contributions increase total expenses depends on the sponsoring bank's overall strategy for balancing the various needs and objectives of the bank.
- The preceding example assumes that balance sheet growth would be identical under all scenarios. However, because the ESOP may provide a greater amount of capital over time, the sponsoring bank may be able to realize greater balance sheet growth in the long

term, thus enhancing shareholder value. For example, by using the ESOP to provide shareholder liquidity, more shares remain outstanding relative to an alternative of repurchasing shares into treasury and thereby reducing common equity.

Tax Considerations

Tax qualification is an attribute bestowed on an employee benefit plan that meets certain requirements. This status allows the plan sponsor to make contributions to the plan using pretax dollars, within certain limits, and also allows the income tax on the participants' benefits to be deferred until the benefits are actually received by the participant or the participant's beneficiary.

For an ESOP to retain its tax qualification, the plan must be designed and operated in compliance with Code and ERISA rules. These rules were created, for the most part, to ensure that plans do not discriminate in favor of highly compensated employees, and that plans are administered to protect the rights and benefits of plan participants. Employers should use experienced professionals to assist with plan operations and compliance in light of the complex body of interrelated regulations.

C Corporation ESOPs

Figure 2-1 shows the relationship between a C corporation bank holding company, the ESOP trust, the employees, and other shareholders. This example depicts the ESOP's purchase of stock from existing shareholders.

Figure 2-1 assumes a direct sale of stock from an existing shareholder to the ESOP. Such transactions are common for small blocks of stock for which the purchase can be funded by cash accumulated in the plan.

ESOP transactions can become more complicated, however. For instance, to purchase shares beyond its existing cash resources, the ESOP may use debt in a leveraged ESOP transaction. In one variation of this transaction, the bank holding company would borrow funds from another bank, and the bank holding company would then loan the funds to the ESOP via a mirror loan. The bank holding company and potentially the seller of the shares acquired by the ESOP would guarantee the third-party bank loan. The bank holding company would

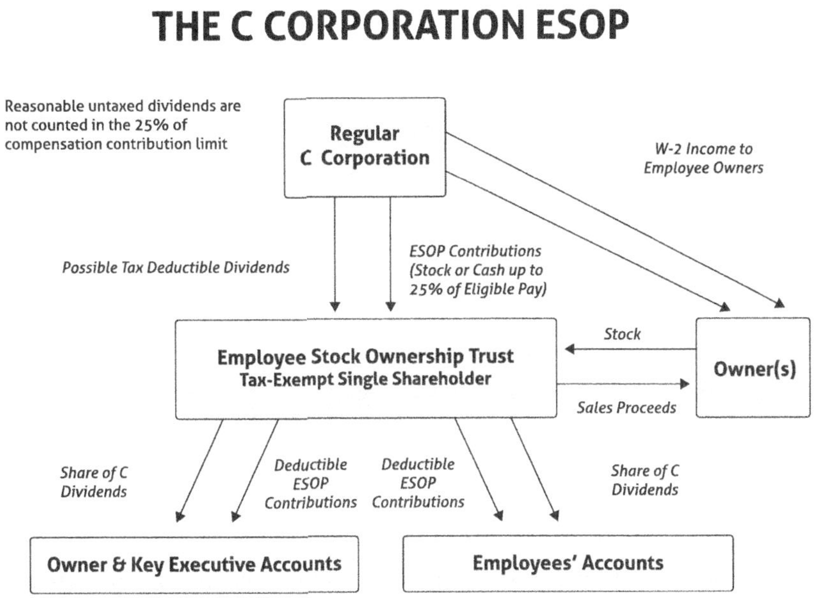

Figure 2-1. ESOP purchase from existing shareholders

make tax-deductible contributions of cash to the ESOP, thereby enabling the ESOP to make debt service payments on the "mirror" loan to the bank holding company, which would then in turn service the third-party bank debt.

C corporation banks and bank holding companies with a large number of shareholders will often have different strategies for stock purchases than S corporations, since more than one class of stock may exist for the C corporation holding company.

A major advantage of private C corporation ESOPs that is not available for S corporation ESOPs is the ability of a shareholder who has held their shares for three years or more to take advantage of a tax-free sale of stock to the ESOP in a tax-free (tax-deferred) rollover under Section 1042 of the Code (see "Rules for Using the Section 1042 Rollover" in chapter 1).

S Corporation ESOPs

An S corporation is a "pass-through" entity in which the individual shareholders are responsible for the income taxation attributable to their pro rata portion of the bank or bank holding company's earnings. The ESOP, like any other S corporation shareholder, participates in the profits and losses of the sponsoring corporation. The ESOP receives its proportionate share of any earnings that are distributed at the direction of the board of directors, computed on a per-share, per-day basis in the tax year under consideration. Since an S corporation ESOP is treated as a single shareholder and pays no taxes, the earnings on S corporation shares held by the ESOP are not taxable. They flow untaxed into the plan and can be used to purchase additional shares or pay down a stock acquisition loan.

The direct pass-through of earnings means that the S corporation ESOP can be more tax-efficient than its C corporation counterpart. At the extreme end of the ownership spectrum, i.e., an ESOP owning 100% of the employer's common stock, the only shareholder is the ESOP trust, which pays no taxes. Therefore, there is no need to distribute earnings on shares to taxable shareholders to cover their tax obligations, and the sponsoring S corporation becomes effectively tax-exempt.

While banks or bank holding companies making the S tax election are not numerous, they do exist and have adopted ESOPs. The number of 100% ESOP-owned companies is increasing, although largely outside of the banking industry.

Figure 2-2 depicts a scenario in which the ESOP purchases stock directly from an existing S corporation shareholder using funds from the plan (either from cash accumulated in the plan or via a seller note whereby the ESOP makes periodic principal and interest payments to the seller).

If the company reports earnings of $1 million and the ESOP owns 50% of the shares, the non-ESOP shareholders, who own the remaining 50% of the stock, would be responsible for the taxes on $500,000 of the company's earnings. The ESOP would not be responsible for any taxes on earnings. A distribution of 35% of earnings to the taxable shareholders to satisfy their income tax obligations would require the same distribution to the ESOP of $175,000. This is a much more efficient method of recovering tax dollars than the corporation making a simple deductible contribution to an ESOP.

To achieve a recovery of tax dollars equal to $175,000 with a pretax contribution of either stock or cash to an ESOP, the required contribu-

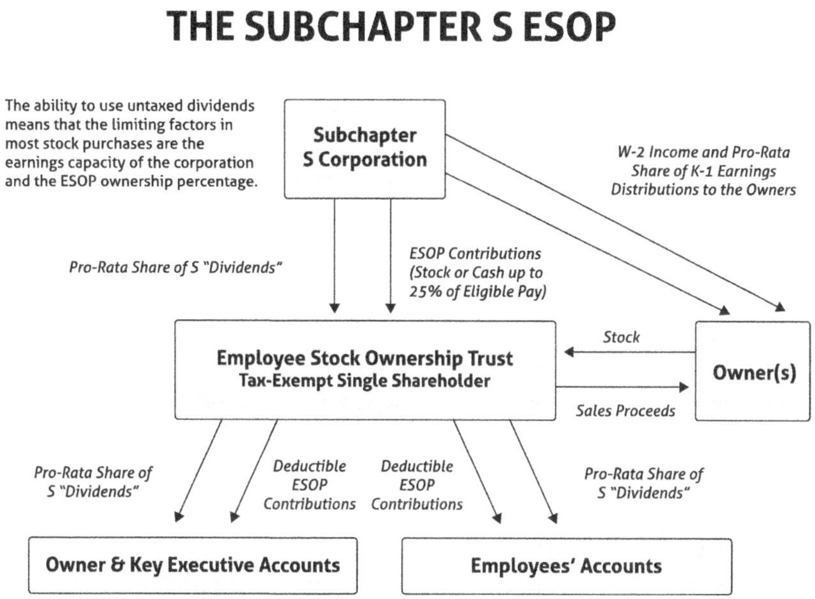

Figure 2-2. S corporation ESOP

tion at an assumed 35% combined state and federal tax rate would be about $270,000 in the case of our 50/50 ownership split between the ESOP and non-ESOP shareholders. The company still distributes cash in the amount of 35% of $1 million, but in this case, the ESOP share of the distribution represents a complete recovery of dollars that would otherwise be lost to taxation.

Despite the substantial benefits of using an ESOP with a large ownership interest to improve cash flow in S corporations, this strategy may be difficult to implement for several reasons. First, the other shareholders want to partake in the earnings. But, more importantly, it takes significant time (typically more than 10 years) for a company to fund the purchase of a significant portion of its shares, even with a full tax shield for the ESOP purchase. Additionally, when an ESOP uses a loan to purchase shares, the debt may have a negative accounting impact on shareholders' equity. In accounting terms, a "contra-equity" account arises because the accounting rules treat the leveraged transaction as if it were a direct repurchase of stock. While the contra-equity account declines over time as the debt is repaid, the transaction would dilute the holding company's capital ratios at the outset. Finally, an

ESOP owning a large percentage of the holding company's outstanding stock may be required to anticipate the future cost to repurchase shares from participants exiting the plan.

There also are some concerns with partial S corporation ESOP ownership and high levels of corporate earnings. For example, if in our example ESOP above only had 40% of the stock and the outside 60% owners wanted 70% of earnings distributed, the ESOP's share of the $1 million of earnings would be 40% of $700,000, or $280,000. That could represent more cash than the ESOP needs for share purchases, loan payments, or repurchases of shares from departing, vested account balances. Some S corporation banks with partial ESOPs have inadvertently "overfunded" their plans as a result of large shareholder distributions to outside shareholders, making for some large participant accounts. This is not common, but represents one of many design considerations when implementing an ESOP.

Additionally, terminated participants who may not have received a distribution of their vested account balances in the ESOP may still have all or a portion of their account held in the form of bank shares; the presence of stock in terminee accounts could benefit both from distributed earnings on their S corporation shares as well as share price appreciation in the underlying shares. The effect of growing account balances for terminated participants is not difficult to deal with but needs to be understood both in the design and ongoing operation of an ESOP.

Very small S corporation ESOPs face an additional concern that C corporation ESOPs do not: the Code Section 409(p) anti-abuse rules. After the passage of legislation in 1998 permitting ESOPs to be eligible shareholders in S corporations, Congress and the Internal Revenue Service (IRS) belatedly recognized that there was a potential for abuse. The concern is that the ESOP would not share ownership broadly on a nondiscriminatory basis, yet would provide a full tax exemption to the selling shareholders who are also the participants in the ESOP receiving allocations of the very shares of stock they sold.

Since any S corporation with all of its shares held in the tax-exempt ESOP trust is effectively an untaxed entity, a small company with few employees could retain its earnings on the untaxed balance sheet of the company with that wealth concentrated in the accounts of just a few

ESOP participants. Concerned about the unintended consequences of such a massive tax shelter, Congress added Code Section 409(p) and the IRS implemented corresponding regulations to prevent such a concentration of ownership. A failure to meet this requirement effectively destroys the ESOP through a 50% excise tax on the amounts held by "disqualified persons," possible disqualification of the plan, or other negative effects.

Although there are ways of addressing the ownership concentration issue, S corporation companies with fewer than about 15 participants in an ESOP, or with a potential of declining to that level, should either convert to C status or consider an alternative to the ESOP.

Limits on ESOP Contributions

For an ESOP, as for any other tax-qualified retirement plan, the IRS imposes limits on the amount of tax-deductible contributions that may be made each year. For eligible participants, typically those working at least 1,000 hours per year and aged 21 or older (though sponsors can be more generous), the contribution by the sponsor to all of its qualified retirement plans each year cannot exceed 25% of "covered" compensation. For example, a bank with an eligible payroll of $2 million, making employer 401(k) contributions of $100,000, could contribute a maximum of $400,000 to an ESOP on a tax-deductible basis. (Total allowable contribution of 25% of $2 million = $500,000. Netting out the 401(k) contribution of $100,000 leaves $400,000 for the ESOP.) Table 2-5 lists the caps for the 2023 plan year.

Table 2-5. Plan limits for 2023

Category	2023 limit
Compensation limit for computing all plan contributions (Code Sections 401(a)(17) and 404(l))s	$330,000
Maximum 401(k) elective deferral (Code Section 402(g)(1))	$22,500
Age 50 401(k) catch-up contribution maximum (Code Section 414(v)(2)(B)(i))	$7,500
Annual addition limit without 401(k) catch-up amount (Code Section 415(c)(1)(A))	$66,000
Annual addition limit with 401(k) catch up above age 50	$73,500

It must be noted that ESOPs have some exceptions to the above limits. For example, the following additional monies flowing untaxed into an ESOP do not count towards any of the above limits:

- S corporation earnings distributed with respect to shares held by an ESOP (which can be used to purchase and repurchase shares or pay down an ESOP loan), and,
- C corporation dividends that are characterized as reasonable by the IRS.

The effect of these exceptions for ESOPs is that the contributions to ESOPs generally exceed that of other profit-sharing plans. For example, the average employer contribution to a 401(k) is about 4% of compensation. We have seen ESOPs in some cases with total funds flowing into participant accounts averaging 35% or more of eligible pay in some years. Though the national average for ESOPs is closer to 8%, the higher level of plan contributions eventually results in substantial stock values accumulating in participant accounts, making the ESOP a great tool for building retirement savings.

Table 2-6 summaries the similarities and differences between S and C corporation ESOPs.

Legal Considerations

Plan Compliance, Recordkeeping and Department of Labor Audits

After the initial implementation of an ESOP, upkeep is needed annually to continue the management of the plan and to ensure compliance with the law. For instance, companies that sponsor ESOPs are required to perform recordkeeping each year to allocate shares of company stock to employees and to inform employees as to the value of shares in their ESOP account, based (in closely held companies) on an independent annual valuation.

For an ESOP, the ongoing compliance process presents some unique requirements. Although an ESOP is a tax-qualified defined contribution plan, there are significant differences from a 401(k) or

Table 2-6. Summary of similarities and differences between S and C corporation ESOPs

Feature	Private C corporation ESOP	S corporation ESOP
ESOP Section 1042 tax-free rollover	Yes, if ESOP owns 30% or more	No
Tax-deduction limit for ESOP loans	Includes only principal in most cases; must pass "one-third" anti-discrimination test for this; otherwise, the limit includes principal and interest	Counts both principal and interest
Tax-deductible dividends	Yes, if "reasonable" and used to retire ESOP debt, passed through to participants, or reinvested in shares	No
Untaxed earnings on ESOP shares	No	Yes
Dividends can be distributed to participants	Yes	No
Retiring participants can demand stock pursuant to put option	Under a special rule, banks with ESOPs are not required to distribute shares if they provide participants with the right to cash distribution for the value of the shares. If a bank's bylaws or charter restrict ownership of substantially all stock to employees or a qualified plan, it can also provide cash distributions in lieu of the right to demand shares.	No
Participants vote their shares	No except in very major issues: liquidation, sale, sale of substantially all of the assets, merger (yes if publicly traded)	No, except in very major issues: liquidation, sale, sale of substantially all of the assets, merger
Tax-deduction limit for combined qualified plans	25% of eligible compensation, not counting dividends paid to ESOP	25% of eligible compensation, not counting distributions on ESOP shares

profit-sharing plan. The employer and trustees must consider the following to ensure documentation and compliance obligations are met:

1. Plan document amendments as required
2. Summary plan description (SPD)
3. Investment policy and actual investment of cash balances
4. Participant education
5. Plan recordkeeping, including analysis of the census and financial data
6. Production of an allocation report that includes financial statements; summary of financial assumptions and transactions (including release of shares of employer stock) for the plan year; results of applicable compliance tests; participant detail, including updated eligibility and vesting; allocation detail in total and per participant, including contributions, forfeitures, distributions, dividends or S corporation distributions, investment gain or loss, and ending balances
7. Participant statements
8. Administrative distribution policy
9. Management of the distribution process including, qualified domestic relations orders
10. Method for funding of plan distributions (stock repurchase obligations)
11. Annual Form 5500 information return series and all related 5500 schedules
12. Plan audit by a CPA for plans with over 100 participants
13. Summary annual report (SAR) for participants

Compliance and administration can be complex and time-consuming. Sponsoring companies should consider retaining professionals to serve as ERISA legal counsel to prepare any required document amendments and address other issues, professional recordkeepers to prepare annual participants' statements and testing, and a CPA to prepare the Form 5500 tax filing and perform the plan audit (if applicable).

The annual information return is due by the end of the seventh month after the plan year-end and is filed with the DOL in conjunction with the IRS.

If an employer's ESOP plan is selected by the U.S. Department of Labor (DOL) or IRS for audit, it does not mean there is an anticipated violation. Records will be requested and reviewed over months and a report issued with any findings of error and mandated corrections. ERISA counsel should be contacted upon receiving notification that a plan will be audited. (See appendix B for a sample copy of a DOL ESOP audit checklist.) If there are operational errors in the administration of the plan, various remedies are available for correction and will be disclosed by the DOL or IRS auditor and resolved.

If an employer is made aware of or discovers an administrative error that is an operational defect and the plan is not being audited by the IRS or DOL, then steps must be taken to correct plan operations and make the plan "whole."

Under an IRS program known as the Employee Plans Compliance Resolution System (EPCRS), plan sponsors and other plan professionals can correct certain errors in employee retirement plans, in some cases without even having to notify the IRS. Correcting plans in this way allows participants to continue receiving tax-favored retirement benefits and protects the retirement benefits of employees and retirees.

EPCRS offers several levels of correction programs:

1. The Self-Correction Program (SCP) permits a plan sponsor to correct "insignificant operational failures" in certain simple plans, such as 403(b) plans, Simplified Employee Pension Plans (SEPs), or SIMPLE IRA plans. These corrections can be made without having to notify the IRS and without paying any fee or sanction.
2. The Voluntary Correction Program (VCP) allows a plan sponsor, at any time before an audit, to pay a limited fee and receive the IRS's approval for a correction of a variety of operational or document-based failures for a qualified plan, a 403(b) plan, SEP, or SIMPLE IRA plan.

3. The Correction on Audit Program (Audit CAP) allows a sponsor to correct a failure or an error that has been identified during an audit and pay a sanction based on the nature, extent, and severity of the failure being corrected.

The VCP and Audit CAP programs are available to ESOPs. A tax and/or legal professional should be involved in the planning of all corrections and filings under the selected program.

What Is a Fiduciary?

Generally, a fiduciary is anyone who has control or direction over ESOP assets. The principal persons who have a fiduciary role in an ESOP are the members of the board of directors, a plan administrative committee, and the trustees of the ESOP, who are appointed by the board. These fiduciaries are personally liable for their roles in operating the plan for the "exclusive benefit of the participants" under Section 404(a)(1) of ERISA.

ESOP Fiduciary Exposure and Fiduciary Liability Coverage

To protect the assets of an ESOP as a qualified plan, plan fiduciaries must be covered by an ERISA bond. The bond coverage amount must be at least 10% of plan assets, up to a maximum amount of $1,000,000 if the plan holds employer stock. This bond protects against liability for potential fund mismanagement by trustees, administrators, and others associated with managing the plan. An ERISA bond is commonly and readily obtained from an insurance company. However, the ERISA bond should not be confused with fiduciary liability insurance coverage. Fiduciary insurance coverage should be broader than just "ERISA liability" insurance. The best coverage will encompass any conceivable discretionary judgment action by a fiduciary and will not provide for a claims retroactive date.

Fiduciary liability exposure and insurance are at times misunderstood because many employee benefit plan decision-makers expect that there is some insurance coverage within the corporate commercial and general liability (CGL) portfolio that will cover this exposure. In reality, not only is there no other insurance coverage available, but unlike D&O liability insurance, which almost always carries a specific exclusion for liability arising out of the ERISA legislation, there is no provision for using corporate bylaw indemnification provisions for the liability imposed by ERISA.

As noted above, there is often confusion as to whether mandatory ERISA insurance for employee dishonesty with regard to plan investments, which is satisfied by the "ERISA bond," is also available to cover other employee dishonesty or whether an employer's general commercial liability coverage also covers a loss related to retirement plans. It is important to understand the different coverages and have the right type and amount of insurance to properly protect the employer.

Additionally, until recently, large fiduciary liability claims were unheard of, and with the demands of employees relating to benefit plan options, enrollment periods, and continuous changes in individual coverage details, many human resource managers devoted their time to issues other than possible liability scenarios.

Many sellers of liability insurance products do not fully understand the nuances of ERISA and fiduciary liability insurance. As generalists, many competent and otherwise well-qualified agents do not have the resources and time to devote to coverage details of fiduciary liability insurance. As a result, many organizations may purchase and maintain the wrong coverage or coverage with relatively low limits when compared to the scope of individual employer exposure.

For many employers, fiduciary liability insurance remains much of a mystery, with respect to both exposure and appropriate insurance coverage. The complexities and impending changes of ERISA legislation have had the effect of increasing the liability exposure of corporate executives, many of whom remain unaware of their exposure and the potential risk to their personal assets.

The good news is that there are specialty insurers working in the area of ERISA fiduciary liability insurance in sufficient numbers to get competitive quotes for the required coverage. ESOP sponsors should take care to review the terms of their CGL coverage to determine whether fiduciary liability coverage is included and, if not, to determine the amount of such coverage that is most appropriate for them.

Some Basic Bank Regulatory Considerations

When considering the purchase of bank or bank holding company stock by an ESOP, attention must be given to the possible application bank regulatory provisions, such as Regulation W of the Federal Reserve ("Reg. W") and the change-of-control provisions of the 1956 Bank Holding Company Act (BHCA) in addition to the provisions of the Code applicable to such plans.

In most instances, a bank holding company will serve as the sponsor of the ESOP, with the bank subsidiary also serving as an adopting employer, thereby covering the employees of the bank. To fund the plan, the bank would "upstream" funds in the form of a dividend or make direct contributions to the ESOP based upon the compensation of its employees. These contributions would be used to purchase stock in the bank holding company.

In some cases, however, the bank may itself be the sponsor of the ESOP for state tax reasons or the absence of a bank holding company.

In general, Reg. W governs transactions between member banks and their affiliates, such as a purchase of assets from an affiliate, extension of credit to an affiliate, investment in securities offered by an affiliate, issuance of a guarantee on behalf of an affiliate, and certain other transactions that expose a member bank to its affiliate's credit or investment risk. For purposes of applying the provisions of Reg. W, an ESOP may be considered to be an "affiliate" relative to the acquisition of stock of a bank. However, Reg. W would not apply to a bank holding company that carries out these transactions with the ESOP as its affiliate.

For purposes of applying the change-of-control rules, even a minority interest ESOP may need to demonstrate that it is not in control of the bank as defined in the BHCA, or the ESOP may be deemed to be a bank holding company itself.

To avoid what is deemed a change of control for a member bank or its holding company sponsoring an ESOP, the trustees of the ESOP will often agree that the plan will not acquire 25% or more of the voting stock or in any way gain control without prior approval from the Federal Reserve. The ESOP is required to play a passive role if the plan is to own from 10% to less than 25% of the voting shares. The passivity commitments may include, among others, an agreement not to seek to exercise a controlling influence over management or policies of the bank, and an agreement not to seek or accept representation on the board of directors. An ESOP transaction can be structured to avoid the characterization of control. While the large majority of bank ESOPs own less than 25% of company stock, there are some 100% bank-owned ESOPs, and they have found the tax benefits well worth the extra regulatory steps.

Other required agreements pertaining to the ESOP's ability to acquire securities include:

- The ESOP will not acquire any security prohibited to the holding company by the BHCA.
- The ESOP will not take on debt that results in the combined debt of the holding company and the ESOP exceeding 30% of the holding company equity without Federal Reserve approval.
- If the ESOP is to acquire more than 25% of a holding company's shares or if counter-dilution could result in an increase in the ESOP's ownership interest to that level, prior approval must be obtained to be a registered bank holding company.

Although the passivity commitments were developed by the Federal Reserve in the context of bank holding company regulation, these principles are of general applicability to investments in nonmember banks and national banks presently regulated by the FDIC and the OCC, respectively, and eventually to be regulated by the FDIC in the case of state-chartered savings institutions and by the OCC in the case of federally chartered savings institutions.

What Securities Can an ESOP Purchase?

The simplest and most general rule is that an ESOP must own the employer security with the highest and best voting rights and dividend preferences.[3] The technical definition of "employer securities" means common stock issued by the employer (or by a corporation that is a

3. Code Section 409(l).

member of the same controlled group) having a combination of voting power and dividend rights equal to or in excess of the class of common stock of the employer having the greatest voting power and the class of common stock of the employer having the greatest dividend rights.

An ESOP sponsored by an S corporation must hold the single class of stock required of S corporations. This is the common voting stock, even though some S corporations have both voting and nonvoting shares (which are not treated as two "classes" of stock). The ESOP cannot buy nonvoting equity.

Many S corporations, in becoming an ESOP company, will recapitalize some or all of the nonvoting shares with voting shares, which are then sold to the ESOP. This is occasionally the case when using an ESOP to consolidate a number of minority, nonvoting equity interests into a single untaxed shareholder (the ESOP).

Closely held C corporations often have multiple classes of stock and hundreds of shareholders. This is an area where a good securities counsel with knowledge of ESOP law is essential. A discussion of the many alternatives of stock that may be issued to the ESOP is beyond the scope of this chapter, but an example will illustrate a few possibilities.

A C corporation ESOP can own a convertible preferred stock with voting rights instead of common voting shares. This would mean that the preferred dividend could be paid only on the ESOP shares, and not on shares held outside the ESOP (if not required on the common voting stock, for example). Dividends characterized as reasonable by the IRS would be deductible to the C corporation sponsor if used to retire ESOP stock acquisition debt. Further, the conversion of the preferred stock to common stock after the full curtailment of the ESOP loan can result in the ESOP ownership decreasing as a percentage of the common equity and the non-ESOP ownership increasing by virtue of the indirect equity kicker.

Another factor to keep in mind is the ability of bank holding companies to both sponsor an ESOP and effect corporate redemptions of their shares. This opens up the option of providing a tax shield for the purchase of classes of stock that the ESOP cannot purchase directly. The holding company redemption of shares ineligible for ESOP purchases is followed by the issuance of new common voting shares to the plan in an amount sufficient to offset the tax consequences of the nondeductible stock redemption.

Appendix A: Dos and Don'ts When Installing a Plan

Do:

- Coordinate the ESOP design with all compensation, employee benefit, key executive plan, and capitalization requirements. This coordination can at times even include a major stockholder's estate plan.
- Ensure that the bank has sufficient profitability to take advantage of the tax advantages of contributions to an ESOP.
- Educate employees regarding their influence on the value being created in the ESOP's stockholdings.
- Engage in the process of managing the interaction and effect of stock flows between the company, shareholders, and ESOP.
- Consider the funding requirements for the ESOP's ongoing stock repurchase obligations and actively manage the balance between the emerging liability and the bank's financial needs.
- Obtain independent appraisals of the fair market value of closely held or thinly traded stock for the implementation of the ESOP and for ongoing ESOP transactions.

Don't:

- Implement an ESOP without discussing the complex issues around plan design with a team of experienced professionals.

Managing the Implementation Process

Implementing a new ESOP prompts many questions, and the plan's investment in employer securities creates a different level of complexity than that found in the typical 401(k) or IRA. As such, expert advice is often needed from a variety of parties to resolve a number of issues. The following identifies a few key steps as well as some key questions to consider to successfully manage the implementation of an ESOP.

- Examine strategic alternatives for the bank and determine whether an ESOP is an attractive option.
  - What are the strategic goals of the bank? Will an ESOP assist and/or complement the bank's strategic objectives?
  - What are the primary goals and objectives for the ESOP? To attract, retain, and award employees? To improve capitalization? To provide a transition strategy for one or more shareholders?
  - What are the potential drawbacks to an ESOP?
  - How does an ESOP compare to other strategic alternatives?
- Gauge interest among stakeholders (senior managers, shareholders, board, and employees) for installing an ESOP.
- Engage a financial advisor to conduct a feasibility study, which typically provides a baseline estimate of the bank's value for the board and management to consider when determining the attractiveness of the plan.
  - Does the financial advisor have the appropriate expertise, (credentials, banking industry expertise, ESOP experience, etc.)? Is the financial advisor independent?
- Engage an experienced ERISA attorney and plan administrator to discuss plan design.
  - Do these professionals have the appropriate expertise (credentials, banking industry expertise, ESOP experience, etc.)? Are they independent?
- Decide whether to proceed with the transaction.
- Determine the transaction structure.
  - How much stock will be purchased?
  - Whose stock will be purchased by the ESOP? Will the stock be newly issued and/or purchased from an existing shareholder?
- Determine the funding mechanism.
  - Will the plan be leveraged, nonleveraged, or some combination thereof?
  - Who will provide the loan if the plan is leveraged? What will the terms of the debt be?

  - How will the additional leverage affect the bank's value (both at implementation and going forward) and financial condition (earnings and balance sheet/capital ratio impact)?
- Determine ESOP trustee and (possibly)the administrative committee
  - Will these roles be filled internally (from an officer or group of employees within the company) or outside the company (attorney or corporate trustee)?
- Determine the strategy, depth, and breadth of employee communications once implemented.
- Appoint the ESOP trustee to engage a financial advisor to render an appraisal upon which the transaction can occur.
- Discuss with your team of advisors the treatment of emerging liability created by the ESOP's obligation to repurchase shares once the plan is implemented.
- Formalize ESOP documents and necessary filings.
- Close the transaction.

Selection of the Advisory Team and Their Roles

Perhaps one of the most important aspects of successfully implementing an ESOP is to assemble a collegial and competent team of advisors. Banking industry and ESOP expertise should be an important consideration when selecting your advisors. Employee benefit plan design and administration is complex and requires the services of a number of professionals.

- *Trustee.* The trustee acts as a fiduciary for the best interest of the plan participants and may be very active in an ESOP. In the context of an ESOP. The trustee is responsible for the purchase of employer securities and the proper maintenance and administration of the plan. When dealing with closely held securities, the trustee has a heightened level of responsibility. For any plan that requires an appraisal, the trustee must select and interact with the appraiser and approve the conclusion of value for securities held by the plan.

- *Third-party administrator.* The administrator is responsible for recordkeeping and may also assist with tax filings and maintenance of plan documents. It is best not to handle the annual plan administration in-house. Engage a third-party administrator with experience in ESOP recordkeeping to prepare the annual trust reconciliation and accounting, the participant account statements, and the filing of the Form 5500 tax return for the plan.
- *Plan sponsor.* The plan sponsor is typically the company.
- *Administrative committee.* Known by a variety of names, an administrative committee is often formed to assist the plan administrator and trustee with various duties associated with the routine administration of the plan and employee interactions.
- *Attorney or plan designer.* The attorney works with the plan sponsor, administrative committee, and trustee to design the plan document and create the documents necessary to implement a stock purchase. Choose a design and implementation advisor who will work with your CPA, corporate counsel, and other existing advisors under a capped fee arrangement—preferably in stages, with at least a cutoff point after a discovery phase.
- *Financial advisor.* The financial advisor may assist the trustee in determining the feasibility of a plan or the fairness of transactions engaged in by the plan from a financial point of view.
- *Appraiser.* The appraiser provides the independent stock appraisals necessary to implement and administer the plan.

Take steps to ensure good communication between your corporate operations, the independent valuation firm, and the plan administrator. Be prepared to deal with complexity and be part of the process. This process has saved many shareholders and companies millions in taxes, made a controlled market for company stock, and rewarded loyal, long-term employees generously.

Appendix B: Department of Labor ESOP Audit Checklist

1. The plan's annual report (Form 5500), including the audited financial statements and the independent auditor's opinion thereon.
2. The current plan document, including any and all amendments.
3. The current trust agreement for the plan.
4. The current adoption agreement, including any amendments.
5. The summary plan description as distributed to participants in the plan.
6. The most recent IRS qualification letter for the plan.
7. The plan's summary annual reports, as distributed to participants for the last three consecutive years.
8. Financial statements, canceled checks, wire transfer statements, and other documents revealing the company's contribution to the plan.
9. The plan's current fidelity bond policy (which identifies the plan as the named insured, carries no deductible, has an amount sufficient to meet ERISA requirements, and includes a one-year discovery period in its general policy provisions).
10. The trustees and plan administrator's fiduciary liability insurance policy(ies) (if applicable).
11. The plan's written investment policies/guidelines (if applicable).
12. Information pertaining to the plan's purchase of company shares. Such information should include:
    a. The characteristics of the company shares (i.e. common stock, preferred stock, cumulative preferred stock, participating preferred stock, stock warrants, stock restrictions, voting, nonvoting, etc.).
    b. The date(s) that the plan purchased the aforementioned shares.
    c. The price paid by the plan for the company stock.

d. The independent appraisals used by the plan's fiduciaries to ascertain that the plan was purchasing the party-in-interest investments at an arm's-length price.

e. The price paid for the aforementioned independent appraisals.

f. The identification of those assets liquidated by the plan in order to purchase this investment (if applicable).

g. The identity of the broker(s) transferring the company stock, if applicable.

h. Document any fees and/or commissions paid by the plan in purchasing and transferring the stock to the plan.

i. If debt was incurred to purchase the employer shares, and this debt remains outstanding, provide the allocation formula and accompanying work product used by the plan fiduciaries to release these encumbered shares to the plan participants in accordance with DOL Regulations Section 2550.408b-3(h). This information should include the plan's amortization schedule; a schedule of payments made to date; a schedule illustrating the appropriate release of encumbered shares to the plan's trust account once payment was received; and the allocation of the encumbered shares to the participants' individual accounts.

13. Information pertaining to the plan's continued holding of company stock. Such information should include:

    a. The plan's rate of return on this party-in-interest investment.

    b. Dividends paid by the company to the plan.

    c. Sales of the party-in-interest company stock from the plan; to include, but not be limited to, the following information:

        i. the date the shares were sold;

        ii. the identification of the purchaser;

        iii. the purchase price paid for the shares;

        iv. the method used by the plan's fiduciaries to determine the purchase price;

        v. the identification of any fees and/or commissions paid by the plan in the selling of the shares; and

vi. the identification of those parties who received fees and/or commissions from the sales of these party-in-interest investments.

14. A list of all company employees; indicate current employees and also provide the date and reason former employees terminated, such as retirement, disability, death, or termination for some other reason.
15. For each terminated person identified above, indicate whether that person received a distribution from the plan, indicate whether the person elected to receive cash or company stock, indicate the date the person was given a distribution, also provide the dollar amount of the distribution.
16. For each terminated person identified above, indicate whether that person exercised a put option, and if so, submit a copy of the put option exercised, the total value of the put option at the time it was exercised (number of shares and amount per share), the determination of the value of the security at the time it was exercised, payment terms, and schedules.
17. Provide a list of all hardship distributions made from the plan; provide a copy of the documentation submitted requesting the hardship distributions, document the review and approval process, and also indicate the amount and date of each hardship distribution.
18. Management letters written to the plan's fiduciaries from the plan's independent certified public accounting firm.
19. Management letters written to the company's board of directors from the company's independent certified public accounting firm.
20. Information pertaining to any private placement or private sale of company stock for the past three years (if applicable).
21. The company share certificates owned by the plan and the percentage of outstanding company shares held by the plan.
22. A list of current company shareholders and the number of shares that they own.
23. Company dividend policies on the stock held by the plan.
24. A list of all company mergers within the last three years that required a shareholder vote.

25. A list of all company consolidations within the last three years that required a shareholder vote.
26. A list of all company recapitalizations within the last three years that required a shareholder vote
27. A list of all company reclassifications within the last three years that required a shareholder vote.
28. A list of all company liquidations within the last three years that required a shareholder vote.
29. A list of all company dissolutions within the last three years that required a shareholder vote.
30. A list of all sales of the company or portions of the company within the last three years that required a shareholder vote.
31. A list of company officers and plan trustees for the plan.

CHAPTER THREE

Valuation for Bank ESOPs

Andrew K. Gibbs and Jay D. Wilson, Jr.

THE PRIMARY ESOP REGULATOR is the U.S. Department of Labor (DOL), which draws its authority from the Employee Retirement Income Security Act of 1974 (ERISA). ERISA requires that an independent third party appraise the stock in a privately held company owned by an ESOP. Secondarily, the Internal Revenue Service (IRS) has authority to review the activities of the plan, given the tax deductibility of contributions. The IRS requires a valuation to be performed annually if the plan is leveraged.

Publicly Traded vs. Non-Publicly Traded Companies

Whether the employer stock is publicly traded can affect the valuation of the sponsor's stock. Often, banks whose stock is listed on an exchange do not obtain independent valuations because the trustee presumes that the value of the ESOP stock will approximate the market price. However, care should be taken by the plan sponsor and the trustee to ensure that the use of the bank's "market" price is appropriate.

The IRS issued guidance on the regulatory definition of "publicly traded" in Notice 2011-19, 2011-11 I.R.B. 550, applying Section 401(a)(35) of the Internal Revenue Code to ESOPs. Section 401(a)(35) was issued in 2010 and defined a company as "publicly traded" if the employer stock is traded on either:

- a national securities exchange that is registered under Section 6 of the Securities and Exchange Act of 1964 (e.g., NYSE or NASDAQ); or
- a foreign national securities exchange that is officially recognized, sanctioned, or supervised by a governmental authority and where the security is deemed by the Securities and Exchange Commission as having a ready market (e.g., the FTSE Group All-World Index).

Stock not meeting the definition noted above, which includes stock traded on the over-the-counter bulletin board or the "pink sheets," would not be considered publicly traded and would be required to satisfy the ESOP requirements that apply to non-publicly traded companies. Additionally, the market price of the stock of certain banks, including those meeting the publicly traded definition described above, may be deemed less meaningful after considering factors such as trading volume, free-float, volatility, and the like.

The Appraiser's Client

The trustee of the ESOP is the independent appraiser's client, rather than the bank or bank holding company. Ultimately, the trustee must review and accept the appraiser's opinion.

When a Valuation Is Needed

The ESOP's need for an independent appraisal arises at several points over its life:

- *Initial valuation for the purchase of stock.* For a new plan, the appraiser may be asked to prepare a preliminary valuation to assess the feasibility and attractiveness of a plan. If a decision is made to proceed, then the appraiser renders an appraisal at a value upon which the transaction occurs.
- *Annual valuation for plan administration purposes.* As an informal rule of practice (unsupported by any formal rule), transactions occurring throughout the year occur at the price determined as of the plan's year-end. For example, transactions occurring

in calendar year 2022 would occur at the appraised value as of December 31, 2021. However, if certain significant transactions occur in the interim, the ESOP trustee may desire an updated valuation of the stock.

- *Periodic valuation for subsequent significant transactions.* If a significant transaction affecting the plan sponsor's stock is anticipated to occur, the ESOP trustee may desire assistance from the independent appraiser. The appraiser can analyze the proposed transaction from a financial point of view and may issue a fairness opinion to the ESOP trustee, which may assist the ESOP trustee in voting the shares held by the plan.
- *Upon terminating the plan.*

Basic Valuation Concepts

Standards of Value

The ASA Business Valuation Standards define the standard of value as "the identification of the type of value being used in a specific engagement; e.g., fair market value, fair value, investment value."[1] The selection of the standard of value drives the application of valuation methods. The most common standards of value include:

- *Fair market value* is the applicable standard of value for ESOP appraisals and is discussed in more detail below.
- *Statutory fair value* is generally defined by judicial interpretation of the relevant statute in a particular state.
- *Fair value for financial reporting purposes* is defined in Accounting Standards Codification Topic 820 as "the price that would be received to sell an asset or paid to transfer a liability in an orderly transaction between market participants at the measurement date."[2]

---

1. American Society of Appraisers, *ASA Business Valuation Standards* (November 2009 revision), "Definitions," p. 31.
2. ASC 820-10-20 (formerly SFAS 157, paragraph 5).

Fair Market Value

Fair market value is the most widely known standard of value and is applicable to almost all federal and state tax valuation matters. Additionally, ERISA defines adequate consideration as, "in the case of an asset other than a security for which there is a generally recognized market, the fair market value of the asset as determined in good faith by the trustee or named fiduciary."[3]

Fair market value has been defined in many court cases, as well as in Internal Revenue Service Revenue Ruling 59-60. Fair market value is defined by the American Society of Appraisers as:

> The price, expressed in terms of cash equivalents, at which property would change hands between a hypothetical willing and able buyer and a hypothetical willing and able seller, acting at arm's length in an open and unrestricted market, when neither is under compulsion to buy or sell and when both have reasonable knowledge of the relevant facts.[4]

The definition of fair market value presumes the following:

- *A willing seller and a willing buyer.* Both are hypothetical parties. Each is assumed to be well-informed about the subject interest and the market context in which it might be transacted.
- *Arm's length.* Fair market value assumes willing, financially capable, and informed buyers and sellers, none of whom is related or acting under any compulsion.
- *Importance of conditions in existence at the valuation date.* Both internal conditions (financial health of subject bank, credit quality, etc.) and external conditions (state of stock markets, the relevant local, regional, or national economy, and industry conditions) must be reviewed and will influence the conclusion of value. From the point of view of fair market value, these conditions and their future outlook should be assessed as of the specific valuation date.

---

3. ERISA Section 1002 (18)(b).
4. American Society of Appraisers, *ASA Business Valuation Standards* (November 2009 revision), "Definitions," p. 27.

- *A focus on the critical three—common sense, informed judgment, and reasonableness.* Revenue Ruling 59-60 states: "A sound valuation will be based upon all the relevant facts, but the elements of common sense, informed judgment and reasonableness must enter into the process of weighing those facts and determining their aggregate significance."[5]

Levels of Value

Valuation theory suggests that there are three general levels of value applicable to a business or business ownership interest. Many writers parse these ideas more precisely. For purposes of perspective, we define the three traditional levels of value as:

- *Controlling interest basis* refers to the value of the enterprise as a whole.
- *Marketable minority interest basis* refers to the value of a minority interest, lacking control, but enjoying the benefit of liquidity as if it were freely tradable in an active market.
- *Nonmarketable minority interest basis* refers to the value of a minority interest, lacking both control and market liquidity.

The traditional levels of value in figure 3-1 shows the relationship between the three levels of value and demonstrates how the indications of value are obtained at each level of value.

Controlling Interest Level of Value

The highest level of value is called the controlling interest level of value. Controlling interest indications of value for banks are commonly obtained directly by reference to actual change-of-control transactions using the guideline transactions method, which is described in the discussion of valuation approaches later in this chapter. Additionally, controlling interest indications of value can be obtained indirectly by reference to minority interest values using a control premium.

---

5. IRS Revenue Ruling 59-60.

TRADITIONAL LEVELS OF VALUE

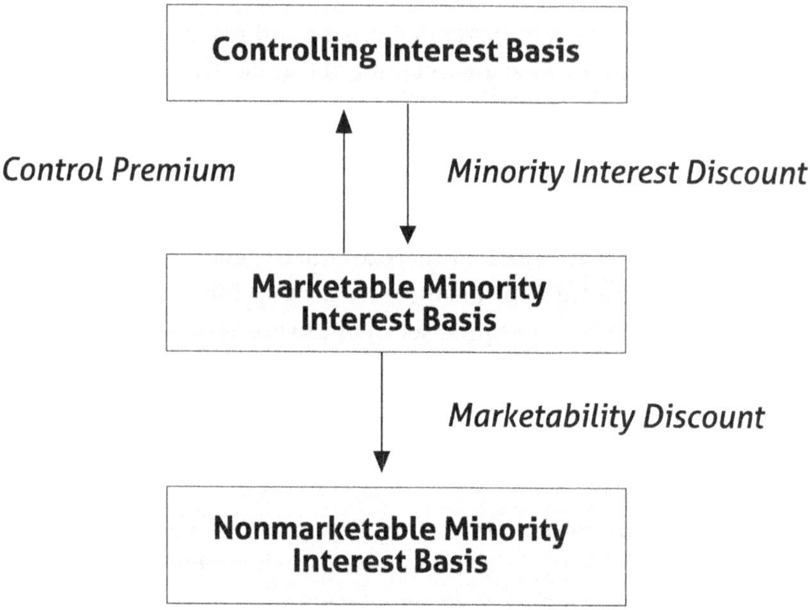

Figure 3-1. Traditional levels of value

The control premium is the difference between the value of a subject interest that exercises control over the company and the value of that same interest lacking control (but enjoying marketability). In practice, the control premium is generally expressed as a percentage of the marketable minority value. When the difference is expressed as a percentage of the controlling interest value, it is referred to as a minority interest discount. Both the concept of the control premium and that of the minority interest discount have been addressed in many studies by appraisal professionals and various court decisions.[6]

Many valuation experts further subdivide the controlling interest level of value into strategic control value and financial control value. We define strategic control and financial control as:

---

6. American Society of Appraisers, *ASA Business Valuation Standards* (November 2009 revision), "Definitions," p. 26.

- *Strategic controlling interest basis* refers to the value of the enterprise as a whole, incorporating the strategic intent that may motivate particular buyers and the expected synergies that may result from an acquisition.
- *Financial controlling interest basis* refers to the value of the enterprise excluding any revenue and expense synergies that may accrue to a strategic buyer. This level of value is viewed from the perspective of a financial buyer, who may expect to benefit by improving the enterprise's cash flow and its capital structure but not through any operating synergies that may be available to a strategic buyer.

Observing the differential between the financial controlling interest level of value and the strategic controlling interest level of value at a specific time can be difficult for a variety of reasons. Generally, a conclusion of value at the strategic controlling interest level of value results in a conclusion of value greater than a conclusion of value at the financial control level. However, a preponderance of financial buyers in a given industry can result in competitive bidding and the acceptance of lower returns by an individual financial buyer, which may increase prices paid by financial buyers to a level comparable to the prices offered and/or paid by strategic buyers.

Marketable Minority Interest Level of Value

The marketable minority interest level of value is typically the reference point for which the other levels are described. Indications of value on a marketable minority interest basis are often obtained by reference to valuation multiples of comparable publicly traded companies using the guideline public company method, which is described in the discussion of valuation approaches later in this chapter. Marketable minority interest indications of value can also be obtained directly by using a build-up methodology, which develops capitalization rates by estimating required rates of return in relation to public markets, or indirectly by reference to a control valuation via the application of a minority interest discount to reflect the lack of control.

Nonmarketable Minority Interest Level of Value

The nonmarketable minority interest value is typically derived by determining value at the marketable minority interest level of value and then applying a discount for lack of marketability. The American Society of Appraisers defines a discount for lack of marketability as "an amount or percentage deducted from the value of an ownership interest to reflect the relative absence of marketability."[7] Thus, a marketable minority interest would be worth more than a nonmarketable minority interest that is identical in all other respects, and the difference between the two (the marketability discount) is due to the inherent risk of holding an illiquid asset. For ESOP appraisals, discounts for lack of marketability generally may be lessened, as many ESOPs contain "put" provisions, requiring the employer or the ESOP itself to repurchase shares of stock from departing employees.

Valuation Approaches

The process of creating a valuation means consideration of various ways of measuring value. The *American Society of Appraisers' Business Valuation Standards* (ASA) recognizes three general approaches to valuation. Within each approach, the appraiser may apply various methods. The valuation methods used are considered by the appraiser to be those most appropriate to the valuation.

Asset Approach

The ASA BV Standards define the asset approach as "a general way of determining a value indication of a business, business ownership interest, security, or intangible asset using one or more methods based on the value of the assets net of liabilities."[8] Asset-based valuation methods include those methods that seek to write up (or down) or otherwise adjust the various tangible and/or intangible assets of an enterprise.

---

7. American Society of Appraisers, *ASA Business Valuation Standards* (November 2009 revision), "Definitions," p. 26.

8. American Society of Appraisers, *ASA Business Valuation Standards* (November 2009 revision), "BVS-III Asset-Based Approach to Business Valuation," p. 9.

Within the asset approach, a potential method used for valuing a financial institution is the net asset value method. The net asset value method develops a valuation indication in the context of a going concern by adjusting the reported book values of a subject bank's assets to their market values and subtracting its liabilities (adjusted to market value, if appropriate). This approach often is less meaningful than the income and market approaches.

Income Approach

The *ASA BV Standards* define the income approach as "a general way of determining a value indication of a business, business ownership interest, security, or intangible asset by using one or more methods through which anticipated benefits are converted into value."[9] Valuation methods under the income approach include those methods that provide for the direct capitalization of earnings estimates, as well as valuation methods calling for the forecasting of future benefits (earnings or cash flows) and then discounting those benefits to the present at an appropriate discount rate. One of the most common methods used to value financial institutions within the income approach is the discounted cash flow method, which relies upon a projection of a future stream of benefits, the present value of which represents the indication of value of the subject bank.

Market Approach

The ASA BV Standards define the market approach as "a general way of determining a value indication of a business, business ownership interest, security or intangible asset by using one or more methods that compare the subject to similar businesses, business ownership interests, securities or intangible assets that have been sold."[10] Within the market approach, the most common methods are:

---

9. American Society of Appraisers, *ASA Business Valuation Standards* (November 2009 revision), "BVS-IV Income Approach to Business Valuation," pp. 10–11.

10. American Society of Appraisers, *ASA Business Valuation Standards* (November 2009 revision), "BVS-V Market Approach to Business Valuation," pp. 12–13.

- *The transactions method.* The transactions method develops an indication of value based upon consideration of actual transactions in the stock of a subject entity. Transactions are reviewed to determine whether they have occurred at arm's length, with a reasonable degree of frequency, and within a reasonable period of time relative to the valuation date. Finally, the transactions should be of a similar level of value (i.e., a limited number of transactions involving a small number of shares would generally be inappropriate for a controlling interest valuation). Inferences about current value can sometimes be drawn, even if there is only a limited market for the shares and relatively few transactions occur.
- *The guideline public company method.*[11] The guideline public company method develops an indication of value based upon pricing multiples of guideline companies. When valuing banks, guideline companies are most often publicly traded financial institutions that provide a reasonable basis for comparison to the investment characteristics of the subject bank. Sifting through the hundreds of publicly traded banks in the United States, appraisers evaluate comparability on the basis of several measures, most notably asset size, geographic location, asset quality, and profitability. The most commonly used version develops a price/earnings (P/E) ratio or price/tangible book value (P/TBV) ratio with which to capitalize net income or tangible book value (total equity, minus goodwill and other intangible assets recognized in business combinations). If the public company group is sufficiently homogeneous with respect to the companies selected and their financial performance, analysts may begin the analysis by calculating an average or median P/E or P/TBV ratio as representative of the group or subdivide the group by other means. If the analyst determines that differences exist between the guideline companies and the subject bank, either in terms of risk attributes or growth outlook, then the analyst may adjust the median or average multiples to account for these differences.

---

11. American Society of Appraisers, *ASA Business Valuation Standards* (November 2009 revision), "SBVS-1 Guideline Public Company Method," pp. 33–34.

- *The guideline transactions method.*[12] Also referred to as the merger and acquisition method, the guideline transactions method develops an indication of value based on change-of-control transactions involving target banks with investment characteristics comparable to the subject bank. Transactions are screened to include only those that occurred within a reasonable period of time proximate to the effective date of the valuation and involve target banks with comparable qualities, including asset size, asset quality, geographic location, and profitability. The most commonly used version develops a P/E or P/TBV ratio that is used to capitalize net income or book value. Other relevant valuation indicators for the banking industry may include the premium to core deposits.

Hot Topics in ESOP Valuation

Leveraged vs. Unleveraged Transaction

The use of leverage often creates complexity and misunderstanding in a variety of ways. First, if the ESOP's stock purchase is financed with debt, the transaction almost certainly will not create capital at the bank holding company level immediately, since American Institute of Certified Public Accountants Statement of Position 93-6 generally does not permit it. This accounting pronouncement should be reviewed with the bank's auditors very carefully before implementing a leveraged plan to avoid any unwelcome adjustments to the bank holding company's equity. Second, the value of the stock may fall after the leveraged plan is implemented, depending upon the treatment of the ESOP debt in the appraisal.

An ESOP can engage in a leveraged transaction involving a minority interest (less than 50% of the outstanding shares) or a controlling interest (more than 50%). When debt is involved, there is the expectation that it will be paid from contributions to the ESOP and possibly the ESOP's share of distributions paid to all shareholders. ESOP appraisers may treat the debt and related contributions in a minority interest ESOP as an increase in employee compensation. Hence, costs rise and value falls, all other things being equal. Value will rise over time

12. American Society of Appraisers, *ASA Business Valuation Standards* (November 2009 revision), "SBVS-2 Guideline Transactions Method," pp. 35–36.

as the debt is paid; however, ongoing contributions to the ESOP will continue to reduce earnings. In a control transaction, appraisers may treat the debt as though it were similar to an externally financed stock acquisition. This is appropriate because the controlling shareholder can sell the company and pay the debt. On rare occasions, the debt can be paid solely from distributions, therefore no reduction in the stock value occurs.

Additionally, the use of leverage can create dilution, which lowers value. Dilution is a reduction in the fair market value per share, which occurs when there is an increase in the number of shares without an immediate, offsetting increase in value due to higher earnings or more capital. In the context of an ESOP, it occurs when: (1) shares are contributed to the plan and a tax deduction is taken for the fair market value of those shares, or (2) newly issued shares are purchased by the plan and the purchase is financed with debt. Dilution is considered in the determination of fair market value at the time of the stock transaction. Dilution should not be confused with the decline in value. Dilution is encountered most frequently when the ESOP purchases, or receives a contribution of, newly issued shares of the bank's common stock. The decline in value sometimes occurs when existing shares of bank stock are purchased from a non-ESOP shareholder with debt.

Discount for Lack of Marketability

Appraisers often reduce the discount for lack of marketability if the ESOP plan document contains a "put" provision that is legally enforceable and financially viable. The put clause allows the participant to put the stock to the plan, to the employer, or both. An appraiser can apply a different discount for lack of marketability to stock inside an ESOP than to shares outside the plan.

One area of controversy involves the purchase of shares by an ESOP that would otherwise be subject to a larger marketability discount. If the ESOP pays the ESOP-appraised value, which is based on a relatively low marketability discount, for shares subject to a larger marketability discount that are held outside the ESOP, some have argued that the ESOP would contravene the requirement that it pay no more than fair market value. That is, shareholders outside of the ESOP should not benefit from selling shares to the ESOP at a price reliant upon the put right accorded only to ESOP participants.

Repurchase Obligation

An emerging repurchase liability is the obligation of the plan or the employer to repurchase shares in the plan. The amount of the repurchase obligation is a function of the value of the stock. Since repurchasing stock takes cash (or capital), the repurchase of shares in a mature ESOP often conflicts with other financial priorities of the bank, such as expansion. That is, capital that the bank may prefer to deploy in expansion initiatives may need to be allocated to redeeming shares held by ESOP participants. The emerging liability is rarely an issue in new plans and may not be an issue for many years. Appraisers differ as to the treatment of a repurchase obligations in appraisals. From bank management's perspective, though, the repurchase obligation means that a greater portion of the bank's earnings may be used to redeem shares from ESOP participants exiting the plan, rather than reinvested in the bank. The ESOP repurchase obligation should not be used to reduce unduly the value of the stock and solve the cash flow problem of a mature ESOP.

CHAPTER **FOUR**

Case Studies of Bank ESOPs

Corey Rosen

AS PREVIOUS CHAPTERS NOTE, banks use ESOPs for a variety of purposes, including helping to provide liquidity for thinly traded or non-traded shares, helping to attract and retain employees, providing a marketing edge for customers, tax incentives and potential balance sheet benefits.

The most powerful application of an ESOP, however, is to help create a high-engagement culture, an atmosphere in which employees feel they are part of a team and have a chance to help identify problems and solutions. The three banks profiled here all excel in this aspect.

Paducah Bank and Trust

Paducah Bank and Trust, based in Paducah, Kentucky, has made employee ownership a core concept in how the company is run. The bank is mostly family-owned and operates as an S corporation. The bank, which opened in 1948, has six locations and 168 employees. In 1997, two of the largest banks in Paducah announced that they were selling to even larger, out-of-state banks. That left Paducah Bank the only locally owned financial institution remaining in Paducah. To remain competitive, Paducah Bank enriched its product offerings and further developed an attitude of total commitment to its customers. The bank looked at ways to engage all employees in helping customers understand its products and services and reemphasized its commitment to its community. In 1991, as part of its plan to create a more innovative workplace, Paducah Bank created an ESOP.

The ESOP is not just a financial benefit, it's part of an organizational culture that seeks employee involvement in generating ideas for sales and service, employee well-being, and community engagement. The ESOP has a 401(k) feature that allows employees to defer into the plan and choose their investments, including company stock. The percentage of the company owned by the ESOP has hovered around 20%. The ownership percentage varies principally due to buybacks upon the retirement of ESOP participants. Sometimes the plan buys back the shares and recontributes them to the ESOP, sometimes the company buys back the shares and retains them for future contributions or to retire them, and sometimes there is a combination of the two. This flexibility allows the company to maintain a targeted annual level of company contributions to the plan.

The plan is not leveraged. The company declares a corporate-wide bonus at the end of the year, an amount determined by performance goals. Half of this amount is included in a payroll cash bonus, while the other half is contributed to the ESOP/401(k) plan to purchase bank stock. The company contribution has averaged several percentage points of pay per year.

"Once each owner-employee understands that they own a piece of the company, then their thought processes and behaviors change. We always promote the concept that with each interaction—with a fellow employee, a customer, or in the community—each one of us should 'think like an owner.' Thus, you do what is necessary to protect corporate assets, serve and assist each customer, and support your co-owners," says Paducah Bank and Trust CEO Joe Frampton. "Such behavior, we believe, leads to profitable growth. Our record of steady, profitable, and growing performance over time supports that belief. Happy owner-employees tend to remain with the bank, reducing recruitment and training expense. Our combined ESOP and 401(k) plan now has even created some employee-owner millionaires. Our longest tenured owner-employee just retired in February after 43 years of service."

Getting Employees Involved

In 2002, the bank initiated a new customer service culture, what it called its "Owners' Commitment." Employees participated in the creation of the company credo, motto, vision, and customer service culture to be the premier provider of financial resources. Part of that was a five-minute standup meeting every day at 8:30 a.m. to go over any developments, ideas, and issues. The bank saw results quickly, with many residents moving their banking services to the bank. There is also a quarterly all-employee meeting.

In 2002 the management team began an initiative to take the company from "Good to Great," modelled after the ideas in Jim Collins's book of the same name. All employees received the book and in discussion groups, talked about how it applied to the bank's culture. Every new employee received a copy of the book and participated in a reading and discussion group as well. In 2003, a Good to Great Council was formed to identify the company's core values, which were presented to the board in 2004 as: people, moral soundness, culture, independently owned, and community involvement. In 2005, the team identified its "hedgehog concept," the things that they believe the company can be best in the world at, which they determined were the ability to attract, retain, and develop customers and employees.

Frampton says that the ways they engage employees has evolved. "Morning meetings have been replaced with high-energy short videos called Turn Up Tuesday. The Good to Great Council no longer operates, but now there is WOW University. Wow U was created in 2019 to enhance the client experience, to challenge the norm of how a community bank serves its customers, and to create the most innovative and energetic atmosphere for our team," he says. "While much of WOW U's focus is on the client experience, the curriculum is created to help our team discover the best version of themselves, creating happiness and an exceptional client experience." Employees are empowered to make decisions, while never losing focus on the client.

Paducah Bank brought Google's Search Inside Yourself Leadership Institute's intelligence training into its workplace to help create a more trusting, effective team and compassionate workplace culture. The result was what they call the "The Seven Pillars of WOW" (WOW is a Paducah Bank theme carried through to customer service, marketing, the website, and its business model). The pillars are: emotional, physical, financial, intellectual, social, occupational and environmental. Twenty-three bank teammates joined together to create the foundations of the WOW Teammate Wellness Initiative, committing to be WOW Being advocates for their own wellbeing and that of each teammate. Together they created the framework of resources within all seven pillars to be offered through the WOW Being Initiative.

The concept has several key elements:

- The ability to recognize, understand, accept, and effectively manage thoughts, feelings, and incoming stressors.
- The ability to deal with a variety of situations and to learn how thoughts, feelings, and behaviors affect decisions, and the alternative of an inability to deal with those situations and the results.
- The ability to respond resiliently and effectively to changing emotional states and effectively cope with a variety of situations, stressors, and disappointments that present challenges and obstacles.

The wellness program includes a mindfulness-based emotional intelligence course, journaling prompts, flexible time off, and paid family and medical leave and an employee assistance program (EAP). The company also offers a matched 401(k) program and generous health insurance options that include preventive care.

The bank has told employees that it is committed to providing a work environment that is congruent with its employees' values and beliefs, is stimulating and inherently fulfilling, and allows leisure time for personal and family commitments and activities, including using an employee's skills and knowledge that contribute to the achievement of the organization's goals and objectives as well as challenges that lead to personal growth.

Unusually, the bank recognizes that money is not just a financial issue. People relate to it in a personal way that reflects their values, goals, and even their spiritual aims. Helping their employees understand that and providing them with generous financial benefits has helped to make them better stewards of their customers' money as well.

All these commitments are noteworthy in themselves, but what really makes Paducah stand out is how much these ideas were driven from the bottom up by employees themselves. It's paying off for the employees, the bank, and its customers.

Phelps County Bank

Phelps County Bank's mission statement is *We are Employee-Owners building relationships with purpose, integrity, and fairness through a commitment to teamwork, education, and growth, believing that contributions of time, talents, and service lead to a better community for all.*

As one of the few 100% employee-owned banks in the nation, Phelps County Bank (PCB) is a true ESOP success story. PCB is based in Rolla, Missouri, along historic Route 66, with four locations and more than 500 million dollars in assets. The bank describes itself as a community bank owned by the employees through an ESOP.

Phelps County Bank was chartered in 1963. Don Castleman was an original stockholder and a member of the board of directors. In 1971, Castleman acquired a controlling interest in the bank, and in 1978 he agreed to sell his stock to a holding company, encouraging the other investors to do the same. Phelps County Bancshares, Inc. was established as the holding company and controlled approximately 80% of the bank's outstanding stock. By 1997, the holding company owned 97% of the outstanding stock.

Emma Lou Brent was named the executive vice president in 1976, and in 1982 she was promoted to chief executive officer. During this time, Brent worked closely with Castleman in the development of the holding company and expanded PCB into neighboring markets with the purchase in 1983 of another small community bank in St. James, Missouri. Brent was instrumental in presenting the idea of a profit-sharing plan to Castleman. After much research and deliberation, she decided to propose an ESOP as a way of transferring ownership of PCB to its employees. Castleman agreed to the plan, and PCB's journey into the world of ESOPs began. Over the next 13 years, Phelps County Bancshares purchased all of Castleman's remaining stock to become a 100% employee-owned bank in 1993.

In its initial stages, the ESOP operated as mostly a financial benefit for employees, but Brent, the new CEO, believed it could be a lot more. She wanted employee ownership to be the cornerstone of the company's culture. Working with the NCEO, she and a team of employees created a model for communicating the ESOP and getting employees involved in sharing ideas to improve performance that many other ESOP companies would follow.

That involved two key parts: a communication committee made up of nonmanagement employees to help explain how the ESOP works, and "The ESOP Challenge" to generate ideas. Employee-owners looked for ways to solve the issues that cost the bank time, money, or loss of business. It was the responsibility of that employee-owner to research solutions and present those to the bank's executive team. Multiple improvements were implemented from that challenge, with cash prizes going to the year's best ideas.

Twenty-nine years later, PCB has more than 100 participants in its ESOP. The bank has paid out the original ESOP participants from the early 1990s, handsomely rewarding those retirees for their years of work and faith in the ESOP model. A significant percentage of the bank's current employee-owners have less than five years of service. To incentivize this younger workforce and recruit talent, PCB increased its ESOP contribution rates, often investing 20% or more.

Unlike the case with a standard 401(k), the employees aren't asked to match even $1 of that annual ESOP contribution. Employee-owners are entitled to an in-service distribution once they have completed five eligible years of service and are offered the option to diversify their assets once they have completed 10 years of participation in the plan and reached the age of 45 or older.

The leadership team understands that retirement can feel "like the distant future," so the bank strives to foster a sense of ownership, so employees feel empowered to solve customer problems, present innovative ideas to improve the business, and enjoy the rewards for their commitment to PCB both now and when they retire. PCB has an open-book management style in which monthly financials are shared with every owner. It also maintains both an ESOP administrative committee and a non-administrative communication/culture ESOP committee to keep the communication flowing.

The ESOP administrative committee has seven members, including all chief officers of the bank and its administrative officer. This committee meets regularly and is responsible for overall plan funding and administration.

The ESOP committee has five members made up of one representative from each branch location of the bank and one member from each floor at the bank's main facility. These members are elected annually by their peers after a week of arduous campaigning during Employee Ownership Month. The ESOP committee is responsible for encouraging a sense of ownership throughout the workplace. The ESOP committee also plans and coordinates education sessions, a family fun night in the summer, the annual shareholders' dinner, and an annual celebration of ESOP Week in October. This committee meets monthly.

New employees are greeted by the welcome chair of the ESOP committee and invited to an educational dinner to learn how the ESOP works and the economic advantages of staying with PCB until retirement. Throughout the year, members of the ESOP committee post "Did You Know" articles to highlight interesting ESOP facts and tidbits. The ESOP committee also creates an electronic newsletter for its intranet that highlights milestone anniversaries, department success stories, and information from the bank's "Random Act of Kindness" program. Each department is assigned a month of the year in which to perform a random nice act for someone, or a group of individuals, in the community.

In October, the ESOP committee celebrates Employee Ownership Month with all employee-owners by doing daily trivia and handing out small gifts. The week concludes with an evening of celebration. The ESOP committee hosts a dinner for all employee-owners and puts together a themed evening where employee-owners play games and receive prizes. Holiday lunches, picnics, and casual get-togethers are held throughout the year.

PCB works hard to improve the community that supports it. In addition to the monthly

"Random Acts of Kindness" program, PCB sponsors a yearly fundraising event called "Take a Stand Against Child Abuse." It includes an art competition held at local elementary schools, with the winner's design being printed on T-shirts that are sold around the community. Other businesses assist by sponsoring the cost of the T-shirts so that 100% of the profits get used locally by various charities supporting children. PCB has families and community organizations host lemonade stands across the entire county for the fundraising event. With the support of the community, Phelps County Bank has raised more than $750,000 for local child abuse prevention programs.

This unique model for banking has been noticed. PCB was voted a "Top Small Workplace" by the *Wall Street Journal* in 2007, had a feature article in Inc. magazine, and has won many local awards, including the including the following "Readers' Choice Awards" given by a local newspaper:

- Best Bank (it received this award every year for more than 10 years)
- Best Mortgage Lender
- Best "Green" Business/Organization
- Best Business (over 15 years)

PCB actively promotes its ESOP structure to state and local elected officials. They are active in many trade organizations, including the Missouri Bankers Association and the American Bankers Association. PCB sent representatives to Washington along with the Employee-Owned S-Corporations of America (ESCA) to meet with legislators about matters important to ESOPs and to make known the important impact ESOPs have on local communities and workers.

PCB's employee-owners specifically focus on educating legislators on the following:

- Benefits of employee-owned S-corporations and viewing them as important constituents
- Appreciation of the significant retirement benefits of S-corporation ESOP companies
- Supporting employee ownership trade associations and ESOP companies when legislation or policies may adversely impact ESOPs
- Supporting legislation to promote and expand ESOPs so that more business owners will transition to the ESOP structure and more Americans can become employee-owners

"Our ESOP has a neat history, but we can't rest on that," says Chief Executive Officer Dominic DeLuca. "Don Castleman, Emma Lou Brent, and those early employee-owners gave us a gift. It is our responsibility to grow that gift and write our own ESOP chapter."

Alpine Bank

Alpine Bank is headquartered in Glenwood Springs, Colorado, on the state's Western Slope, and by year-end 2022 will operate 39 locations throughout 30 communities across the state with the new additions of the Colorado Springs and Fort Collins branches. Alpine was started in 1973 as Roaring Fork Bank in Carbondale, Colorado, eventually changing its name to Alpine Bank. The bank has $6.2 billion in assets and 826 employees. It has both Class A voting shares and Class B non-voting shares. The Class B shares trade on the OTCQX Best Market under the symbol "ALPIB."

Alpine Banks's employee ownership culture starts with its mission statement: "To help our customers, employees, shareholders, and community members achieve their dreams." From this, the bank built a framework with the core values of community, compassion, loyalty, integrity and independence.

Employees live and breathe these values, and as a result, the bank has received numerous awards over the years, including being named as the Best Bank and Best Mortgage Broker in 2020 as part of *ColoradoBiz* magazine's Best of Colorado Business Choice Awards.

Corporate social and environmental responsibility is a primary tenet at the bank. Three major initiatives within the bank highlight this commitment—the Green Team, the loyalty debit card program, and paid volunteer time.

- *The Green Team:* In 2006, the bank's Green Team was developed to promote a healthy, clean environment for employees, customers, shareholders, and communities. "Being green and sustainable isn't just about reducing carbon levels or water use," says Vice Chairman/President Glen Jammaron. "It's got to make sense from an overall standpoint: for the bank and for the community. Things like reusing and recycling. Sustainability is really a return to many sensible practices that a lot of people did for generations." Alpine Bank is the only financial institution in the U.S. that has earned the International Standards Organization (ISO) 14001 certification, a globally recognized standard of excellence for environmental management. It was named a Gold Leader at the 15th annual

Environmental Leadership Awards and has been inducted into the International Green Industry Hall of Fame. The Independent Community Bankers of America (ICBA) selected Alpine Bank as the Grand National Award winner for its Community Solar Garden program for low-income families. The American Bankers Association recognized Alpine Bank for the bank's Community Solar Program, which donates bank-purchased solar panels to a local nonprofit to help low-income communities.

- *Loyalty debit card program:* With this program, the bank donates $.10 for every debit card transaction to causes its customers choose. The beneficiaries range from education to arts to Children's Hospital in Denver. Alpine Bank employees are very proud to be part of this corporate culture, and it has played a large role in Alpine's consistently being among the top three corporate donors in the state of Colorado.
- *Paid volunteer time:* In addition to the Green Team and the Loyalty Debit Card Program, paid volunteer time for all employees demonstrates the commitment Alpine has to the communities it serves. Employees give generously of their time and talents using the 24 hours of paid volunteer time, which is allocated annually. This allows employees and their families to support their communities and the causes for which they are passionate.

Employees own 18% of Alpine Bank through its ESOP. The bank's founders, J. Robert Young and William Vollbracht, learned about the virtues of ESOPs in 1983. Although the plan design was relatively new and the true long-term benefits had yet to be seen, sharing the wealth with employees who worked to help build a successful company, and providing a sense of ownership, felt like a good match for the culture they were creating. Employees, directors, and their families owned another 59% of voting shares through individual ownership as of late 2021. Employees purchase Class B shares via the OTCQX.

The bank takes the ESOP seriously. The company makes a discretionary contribution to the plan each year as approved by the board of directors. Historically, this has been 7% of eligible pay and is a very important part of the overall compensation and benefits package at

Alpine Bank. The bank's president hosts a monthly employee owner call updating all employees on monthly performance, progress toward annual goals, and other key indicators.

The bank also offers a 401(k) as an opportunity for employees to save their own money for retirement. Although the company chooses to focus its contribution dollars on the ESOP component and does not offer a match for the 401(k), it has been an incredibly popular benefit plan.

"Very few companies out there can say they're employee-owned," says Shelbi Bauer, Assistant Vice President. "Because of their ownership interest, employees typically report that they have a high satisfaction level with their work and gratification in their role with the bank." That means less turnover.

Of the 74 employees who were in the ESOP when it was established in 1983, 9 are still involved with the bank either as current employees or directors. The average tenure for employees is 6.1 years of service, and the average tenure for officers is 13.5 years of service. Of the 826 employees and officers, 155 have worked for the company for 15 or more years. Juliette Gutierrez, an Alpine Bank employee since 2009, said that it was obvious that when she started working at Alpine Bank that the ESOP was an important benefit to employees. "It didn't take me long to realize the value of being an owner," says Juliette. "Being young and having ownership within Alpine Bank is an amazing feeling that will help me greatly in my future planning."

The ESOP is more than a retirement plan—it's a fundamental part of the bank's culture. The Employee Owner Connection (EOC) (originally known as the Employee Owner Council) was established in 1993 to provide employee involvement in the direction and success of Alpine Bank and to elevate the bank's customer service offerings. Each location and department designate one employee to participate in this group. Members of the EOC are referred to as EOC Ambassadors. These ambassadors serve as the liaison between their department or location and upper management. EOC is a forum to bring new ideas and suggestions regarding the bank and its offerings, as well as a focus on ways to provide top-notch customer service. EOC strives to provide Alpine Bank staff the resources they need to be happy, knowledgeable employees who provide exceptional service to customers. The EOC meets quarterly and is led by a member of the marketing team and a senior banking officer.

J. Robert Young as chair originally adopted these programs and policies of giving back to the community and engaging employees with the ESOP because he thought it would be good for the bottom line. He has since been quoted as saying, "It isn't *good* for the bottom line—it *is* the bottom line."

ABOUT THE **AUTHORS**

Michael Coffey is the president of Corporate Capital Resources, responsible for structuring stock transactions and key executive benefit packages. He has been instrumental in structuring over $200 million in stock sales, transfers, and gifts for the owners of closely held corporations to family, key employees, and public/private charitable concerns. His work over the past 15 years has focused on tax-favored transactions for business continuity, estate plans for private shareholders and their families, and charitable gifts. Michael has published many articles on employee ownership issues and has addressed many national forums on tax-advantaged business perpetuation.

Andy Gibbs leads Mercer Capital's Financial Institutions Group. Andy provides valuation and corporate advisory services to financial institutions for purposes including ESOPs, mergers and acquisitions, profit sharing plans, estate and gift tax planning, compliance matters, and corporate planning. Andy has extensive experience working with financial institutions in merger and acquisition advisory engagements. He has assisted buyers in evaluating the attractiveness of acquisition candidates, determining a price for the target institution, structuring the transaction, and evaluating different forms of financing. For sell-side clients, Andy has analyzed the potential value that the institution may receive upon a sale, assisted in locating potential buyers, and participated in negotiating a final transaction price and merger agreement. In addition, Andy directs projects related to the valuation of intangible assets under Accounting Standards Codification (ASC) 805 and impairment testing under ASC 350. Andy is the coauthor of *The Bank Director's Valuation Handbook: What Every Director Must Know About Valuation*, with Jay D. Wilson, Jr., and *Acquiring a Failed Bank: A Guide to Understanding, Valuing, and Accounting for Transactions in a Distressed Environment*, published by Peabody Publishing, LP.

William Gust is a tax partner at Gentry Locke Attorneys, where he specializes in business, employee benefits, tax, and estate planning. Bill has been assisting closely held corporations in developing and integrating business succession and estate plans for over 40 years.

As part of the process, Bill works closely with allied professionals in banking, insurance and financial services industries. Bill actively represents over 80 ESOP companies nationwide and is a regular speaker on topics involving tax and ERISA strategies.

Corey Rosen is the NCEO's founder and former executive director and now is its senior staff member. Corey has spoken on various subjects related to employee ownership all over the world with government, business, and union leaders, and he is regularly quoted in leading magazines and newspapers. He has appeared on national television and radio programs and also has authored several books on employee ownership, plus more than 100 articles for various business, academic, and professional publications. He has authored or coauthored several of the NCEO's practical and research publications. He holds a PhD in political science from Cornell University.

Jay Wilson is a senior vice president and a senior member of Mercer Capital's Financial Institutions and FinTech Group. Jay regularly works on valuation and merger and acquisition engagements for financial institutions and FinTech companies. He is involved in valuing financial institutions and FinTech companies for a variety of purposes, including ESOPs, mergers and acquisitions, profit sharing plans, estate and gift tax planning, compliance matters, and corporate planning. Jay also has extensive experience providing public and private clients with fair value opinions and related assistance pertaining to estimating fair value marks for financial assets (loans, core deposit intangibles) and liabilities (CD portfolio), goodwill and intangible assets, stock-based compensation, and other financial assets and liabilities. Jay publishes articles on the community bank and FinTech industry and is the author of *Creating Strategic Value Through Financial Technology* (John Wiley & Sons, 2017). Jay also is a coauthor of *The Bank Director's Valuation Handbook: What Every Director Must Know About Valuation*, with Andrew K. Gibbs, and *The ESOP Handbook for Banks: Exploring Alternatives for Liquidity While Maintaining Independence* (Peabody Publishing, LP, 2011).

ABOUT THE **NCEO**

The National Center for Employee Ownership (NCEO) is a nonprofit organization that has supported the employee ownership community since 1981. Our mission is to help employee ownership thrive. We have more than 3,000 members because we help people make smart decisions about employee ownership, with everything from reliable information on technical issues to helping companies reach the full potential of employee ownership. We continuously work to:

- produce practical resources for employee-owned companies;
- conduct research on ESOPs, including showing the economic benefits of employee ownership;
- facilitate the exchange of best practices at our live and online events;
- feature the best and most current writing by experts in our publications;
- advise lawmakers on the best ways to encourage employee ownership;
- help employee ownership companies build ownership cultures where employees think and act like owners;
- and do much more—join today if you are not already a member.

Membership Benefits

NCEO members receive the following benefits and more:

- The members-only newsletter *Employee Ownership Report.*
- Access to the NCEO's members-only website resources, including the ESOP Q&A, the ESOP Lender Directory, and more.
- Access to downloads of sample documents and checklists on essential ESOP topics.
- Free access to both live and recorded webinars.
- Networking opportunities at educational events.

- Discounts on books and other NCEO products and services.
- The right to contact the NCEO for answers to questions.

How to Join or Order This Book

To join or order publications, visit us online at www.nceo.org, where you also can find a wide variety of resources on employee ownership.

To order this book, go to www.nceo.org/r/banks (if you are not already a member but join in the same order, you will receive the member discount on the book).

Made in United States
North Haven, CT
03 November 2026

21721414R00049